When We're Born We Forget Everything

When We're Born We Forget Everything

A Memoir

Alicia Jo Rabins

SCHOCKEN BOOKS
New York
2026

FIRST HARDCOVER EDITION PUBLISHED
BY SCHOCKEN BOOKS 2026

Published by Schocken Books, a division of Penguin Random House LLC, 1745 Broadway, New York, NY 10019.

Schocken Books and the colophon are registered trademarks of Penguin Random House LLC.

Library of Congress Cataloging-in-Publication Data
Names: Rabins, Alicia Jo author
Title: When we're born we forget everything : a memoir / Alicia Jo Rabins.
Description: New York : Schocken, 2026.
Identifiers: LCCN 2025011048 | ISBN 9780593702161 hardcover | ISBN 9780593702178 ebook
Subjects: LCSH: Rabins, Alicia Jo | Jewish women—United States—Biography | LCGFT: Autobiographies
Classification: LCC BM755.R175 A3 2026 | DDC 296.3092—dc23/eng/20250917
LC record available at https://lccn.loc.gov/2025011048

penguinrandomhouse.com | schocken.com

Printed in the United States of America
1st Printing

The authorized representative in the EU for product safety and compliance is Penguin Random House Ireland, Morrison Chambers, 32 Nassau Street, Dublin D02 YH68, Ireland, https://eu-contact.penguin.ie.

בס״ד

To my ancestors who carried our
traditions for so many generations,
and passed them down to me;
to my fellow workers in song;
and to אהרן מיכאל*—always.*

I'm going home without this costume that I wore.

—LEONARD COHEN

When We're Born We Forget Everything

Prologue: The Bathroom Prayer

According to most of the planet, the second millennium was in its waning months. Soon the calendar would reset to zeros. At that moment, the newspapers said, there was a decent chance all the lights in the world would go dark. But we weren't worried. In our calendar, we were smack in the middle of the year 5760—just another in the long, sacred crawl of human history.

This was why we'd come to Jerusalem: for a new way of understanding the world, and our place in it. We each had our own approach, our own reasons. Some of us were acolytes, others rebels; some held a newfound certainty that shielded us like a tortoise's shell, others questioned until the edges of our selves dissolved. What connected us was our shared longing. For God, or ritual, or peace; for comprehending where we'd come from, or divining who we wanted to become.

And so from around the world we gathered, drawn by the magnet of our ancient tradition, to study in a bright open room above a car dealership. Together we memorized the halacha: the Path, the laws, the rules. Together we learned to walk inside that invisible labyrinth of force fields, through which our ancestors had also walked, which stretched out from our bodies and carried us through time.

We tore toilet paper before sundown on Friday so as not to perform the forbidden labor of ripping on Shabbat, stacking the strips on the backs of the toilets in our tiny, musty Jerusalem bathrooms. Before eating bread, we washed our hands with soap, then picked up the two-handled washing urn, pouring the water over our fingers in the kabbalistic tradition, three times for each hand. After each meal, we chanted our thanks for a full five minutes, in harmony.

After using the bathroom, too, we paused in gratitude, standing just outside the door to whisper a prayer praising the Divine for our bodies. Most Orthodox Jews had this blessing memorized, but in our yeshiva, a laminated printout was taped to the wall next to the bathroom. *If even one artery or passageway were to be stopped up, it would be impossible to stand before you and praise you, O God.*

Some of us had grown up, like me, in secular Jewish homes. Others had converted, traveling even farther from their families of origin. A few had been raised ultra-Orthodox; most people who left that community headed to secular life, but a handful found their way here. Some of us were skeptical, some angry, some lighthearted, some filled with unquestioning faith. Some of us would go on to be rabbis; some would return to our previous lives and pick up where we'd left off.

A space like this, in which people of all genders studied Torah side by side, would have been inconceivable in previous centuries. Together we read the stories of our forefathers (*covenant, father of multitudes, he to whom God speaks*) and foremothers (*helper, beautiful, mother of all living*). We lovingly dissected the words of the ancient rabbis, who retold the biblical stories with fiery creativity and explored the spaces beyond binary gender (*androginus, tumtum, aylonit, saris*).

And together we studied the sages' words about the dangers of women studying their words (*He who teaches his daughter Torah, teaches her licentiousness*) along with the dissenting opinions (*When a woman is ready to receive an abundance of wisdom, withholding it will harm her*). There were always dissenting opinions, we were learning. Sometimes, I noticed, the dissenting opinions named what I myself believed to be true.

One week in class, we discussed the concept of omnipresence: if God is everywhere, every single thing we do, large or small, is witnessed by the Divine. At lunch afterward, my friend Natalie sat down next to me, looking worried. Her curly black hair grazed my cheek as she leaned in, almost whispering. *I mean, does that mean God is watching while I'm home, like, scratching my butt? Because I really don't want to scratch my butt with God watching. But sometimes I need to scratch my butt.* We discussed earnestly. Was God a separate presence, observing the butt scratching, or was God also the butt, and the finger that scratches, and the itch itself?

Throughout my twenty-one years on this earth, people had repeatedly told me I was *too sensitive.* In yeshiva, no one ever said that. All day, we spoke openly about the sacred, as if it were normal. We walked in everyday magic, linked through the letters of the holy books to the millions of others who had felt this magic too. In the glow of this attention to each moment's sacredness, the sensitivity that had haunted me my whole life finally made sense—an asset rather than a liability.

Maybe, I thought, I could stay here forever. If I followed the rules closely enough—if I dedicated my whole self to what was beyond me—perhaps, in this new way of living, I could finally escape my own loneliness.

Part I

The Garden of Earthly Delights

My grandfather shortened his last name to sound less Jewish, but really, I should have been born Alicia Jo Rabinowitz. Rabinowitz: son of the rabbi. Somewhere in my past there was an old bearded man, probably more than one, and likely some wise women too. Culture bearers, teachers of the tradition. But that was a long time ago.

There are two ways to look at my story.

You could say I was a white American girl growing up in late twentieth-century secular suburbia, sensing a mystery pulsing beneath the sameness of number two pencils, plastic hairbrushes, school buses with their green vinyl seats. In this story, I left everything I knew to search for meaning; I found it in an ancient tradition; and then I had to decide how to come back and live with what I'd learned.

Or you could say I was a Jewish girl born in the Diaspora, in the Hebrew year 5737, whose ancestors improbably passed the traditions on from generation to generation for thousands of years until they reached me, so that I carried within myself the barest forms of ritual (a silver cup, grape juice, the Shema prayer), the faintest Hebrew letters, hints of almost-forgotten languages. In this story, I returned to the faint flame burning inside me.

Either way: God was nowhere in my childhood, but mystery was everywhere.

~

It was the 1980s. Our dining room was cozy: a wooden hutch, plates with blue and red flowers, walls painted peach pink. Across from my seat at the table hung a reproduction of Hieronymus Bosch's ornate painting *The Garden of Earthly Delights.* I stared at it every night during dinner: a packed dreamscape of bodies and spires, pleasure and torture; a moss-green and mahogany panorama of mortal and Divine.

My father came in the front door from the teaching hospital, where he was a psychiatrist specializing in Alzheimer's, depression, and dementia. He put down his dark leather briefcase, loosened his bow tie, hung up his jacket, and sat down as my mother called, "Dinnertime!" to me and my two younger sisters.

My mother, her hands in quilted mitts, carried a Pyrex dish of steaming lasagna from the oven. White strands were just beginning to appear in her short black hair. Between bites of buttered peas, we laughed, teased each other, and reported on our days.

My father loved his work, and he would often tell us stories about memory. We knew about Phineas Gage, the railway worker who miraculously survived when a tamping spike blew through his brain and out his head in 1848, but who was left with a greatly changed personality and severe memory loss. ("Gage was no longer Gage," a friend of his reportedly said.) We knew about H.M., who lost his short-term memory on an operating table in 1953, when a surgeon removed both of his hippocampi in an attempt to cure his epilepsy. *H.M is still alive,* my father said. *They use his initials to protect his privacy. They study him at MIT.* He shook his head. *It's tragic, but it's also a great service to the medical profession. He doesn't know whether his parents are alive or dead, but everyone says he's a very sweet man.*

Questions were a currency of love in our house. My sisters and I listened intently to my father's mini-lectures; the more insightful our questions, the more delighted he grew. *That's a very good point,* he would say. *And that's exactly why every experiment needs a control.* His dark eyebrows rose as if pulled by strings, his voice creeping up in volume, louder and louder.

And every time I looked up, *The Garden of Earthly Delights* pointed me again toward that mystery, that nameless power I sensed just outside the walls of our cozy house. No one had spoken directly of this power, yet I felt it: the cold black river of night; dreamlike bird-monsters; death, loss, the exquisite terror of knowing everything I loved would end.

I sat back and let the words blur into sounds as my family talked around me. Butter melting on peas, love reverberating in the room, the enigma of the human brain, the way questions could bind us together. We had everything we needed, so why did I feel a hole at the center of it all?

For me, this mystery was a form of loneliness.

∾

Some of my friends' families said grace before dinner: *Jesus, thank you for this food.* I found this exotic and uncomfortable, since my family just sat down and ate. But when it came to the holidays, I knew that we were the exotic ones, our family menorah on the mantel a weak substitute for the glowing Christmas tree that filled every other window on the block.

Growing up Jewish in an almost entirely Christian suburb

meant that Jesus was palpable, but mysterious—the ruler of an adjacent, vaguely threatening empire, under whose auspices we lived. God was less foreign, since we heard about Him (always "Him") the few times a year we went to synagogue. But even God was blurry: a great-great-grandfather whose name we couldn't quite remember, who spoke a language we didn't understand, probably believed the earth was flat, and wouldn't approve of the way we lived.

God was indistinct to me, but mystery was clear; it surrounded me on all sides. In the slice removed from H.M.'s brain that cured his seizures but left him unable to form new memories, and in the seventeen-year cicadas that emerged that spring from their tunnels in the ground, shedding their shrimplike shells across the concrete sidewalks. Mystery lived in our small, sloped backyard, its built-long-before-we-moved-here steps of mica and falling-down stone walls barely visible beneath spreading ivy and pachysandra. The impossible sweetness of coming together in that dining room together night after night, year after year, the peacock-feather fan hanging from the window frame, the doorbell that rang sympathetically when my dad raised his voice in excitement—as if there were a ghost in the room.

When I was ten, I made up my own definition for God. *God is everything science has not solved yet,* I wrote in my notebook. We were not deluded believers in some father figure; we were modern people and we put our faith in science. Yes, I felt mystery acutely, but God and mystery were two different things: so I believed, with the unquestioning faith of a child.

But every childhood ends.

According to tradition, Abraham went forth from the land of his birth to forge a new relationship with the Divine. He smashed the idols of his father, and in the wake of that destruction he began at last to experience God as One. And according to tradition, when Abraham grew up and became a father himself, that same God instructed him to prove his allegiance by binding his own son to be sacrificed on the mountain.

I wonder if Isaac, in that moment, questioned the faith of his father, too. As I hope my children question mine.

Bat Yiftach

(Book of Judges)

The book of Judges tells the story of a girl. We don't know her name, only her father's, so we simply call her "Jephthah's daughter" in English—in Hebrew, Bat Yiftach.

Her story does not end well, at least not on the surface; perhaps this is why it's not often told. The shocking harshness of this narrative, in which a young girl loses her future because of a few capricious words spoken by her father, is not easy to read. It is a tragedy, a cautionary tale, and it goes like this:

Yiftach is a not-very-brave warrior who finds himself in a dangerous battle. Surrounded by the enemy and panicking, he vows that if he is victorious, he will sacrifice the first creature he sees when he returns. And it works, at first; Yiftach wins. But when he arrives back home, he sees his daughter, who has come out to greet him in the traditional way, drumming and dancing.

Yiftach falls to his knees, crying out to her, *I have made a promise to the Lord.* He tells her what he has vowed. Perhaps he is asking her to run away, to riddle him a way out of the vow? Or is he as helpless and foolish as he seems?

Either way, Yiftach's daughter—who does not seem to have a mother, at least not a present one—accepts this news of her fate calmly. *My father,* she answers, *you have given your word. But before you fulfill your vow, let me go with my friends and mourn my virginity for two months. Then I will return, and you must do to me what you have promised.*

This story parallels another famously heart-wrenching one, from Genesis, in which God commands Abraham to sacrifice his son Isaac. There, too, both parent and child seem unable to resist their terrible destinies, though Abraham is less honest with Isaac about his fate than Yiftach is with his daughter.

But there are differences, too, between these stories—major ones. In Genesis, the child in danger is Isaac, a boy with the dignity of a name; here, it's an unnamed girl, daughter of an apparently single dad with poor decision-making skills. In Genesis, God is a chess player, directing pieces across the board; here, the characters seem to be the ones calling the shots. In Genesis, God saves Isaac by providing a ram in his place; Isaac may be traumatized for life, but he lives, and becomes the father of a civilization. Here, it's clear that the vow is fulfilled; no dramatic rescue occurs at the last minute. In Genesis, Isaac grows into a beloved forefather, named three times a day in Jewish prayer—but we don't know Yiftach's daughter's name or future, and her story is rarely told.

But the difference I find most compelling between Isaac and Yiftach's daughter, which calls me back to this story again and again, is the question of why she returns to her father.

After all, anyone who can live for two months away from home can stay away forever. But she does not choose to escape. She has more of a voice than Isaac, and what she says is, *I will return.*

Why?

I suspect (I fear) the answer is faith.

Her God is a child's God, who requires absolute obedience and allows for no mistakes. Her faith is a terrible faith, that of a child taught to believe in an absolute and contradictory God.

This version of the Divine grants us a terrible responsibility—to decide, with our necessarily limited human understanding, who God would have us kill. This Divinity is so unbroken that it must break us. Bat Yiftach's faith is the faith of Isaac's father, Abraham, who hears the commandment to offer his son on the mountain, and arises early in the morning to carry out the sacrifice.

My own young faith, too, was absolute and contradictory, though (thankfully) I was faithful to a different doctrine. God did not exist; that's what I'd been taught, and I was a good student. I was a good girl. I hadn't yet begun to wonder: *What* haven't *I been taught?*

It's not clear what happens to Yiftach's daughter in the story, as if the Torah itself can't bear to say the words. In the most troubling reading, she is literally sacrificed. But the Hebrew is unclear; the language itself seems anxious to avoid naming exactly what happens. And there are the seemingly incongruous references throughout the story, including her "bewailing her virginity" with her friends, which leads Sephardic tradition to interpret that Bat Yiftach returned to be offered as a sort of nun, never allowed to marry or have children, but not literally sacrificed.

Either way, this is a brutal story. And the part of me that loves this character, the part of me that feels certain we'd have been friends—well, I wish she had run away instead of returning to fulfill her father's vow.

But in her choice I recognize my own youthful, headstrong commitment to truth. I suppose she had to follow the path only she could see, as I had to follow mine. And I permit myself the interpretive license we all have, as we read these stories and make them our own.

Perhaps she did not surrender to her father but, instead, to her own adult self. Perhaps Bat Yiftach knows she has to let her child-self die in order to discover what comes next.

Young Magic

Baby powder, vegetable oil, water, clover petals soaked in salt water, crushed tangy clover leaves, oregano, thyme. Ten years old, I stirred these potions in Dixie cups with a thin stick, whispering to myself—rhymes, wishes, incantations—then poured the liquid out carefully beneath a tangle of ivy. I sought out those overgrown suburban corners, where wildness was almost tamed but not completely, and found in them laboratories of magic.

The membrane between life and death is thin. I knew it even then: this is the deal we strike when we're born. So I was afraid of anything that might sweep me under, take away my self-control. Rabies, most of all, which would make a person foam at the mouth and bite their own family. This fear was not entirely unfounded; raccoons rummaged through our trash at night, bats occasionally found their way into the house during humid August dinners when the screen door was left open, and either could have been infected. My father would chase them out, hollering and waving a broom at the ceiling to protect us from the disease they might carry, while my sisters and I squealed and cheered.

My fear of tsunamis, though, was not justified; we lived two hours inland, at the very tip of the Chesapeake Bay. Still, I dreamed night after night of being pulled down by a massive wave.

And, though my parents hardly drank, I was terrified of alcohol. I'd been herded into the auditorium with my fellow elementary school students to watch an anti-drinking film at a school assembly—a mother slurring her words, pearls, cigarettes, a car accident, flames. After that, I would shudder when my father poured a glass of wine at dinner, and for a time I refused to eat in a restaurant that contained a bar. The amber bottles lined up, reflecting gleaming lights: threatening, incendiary, waiting to be ignited.

My father called these fears *anxiety.* "Don't be a worrywart, or you'll end up like your Grandma Lee," he would say. Not his mother, Sylvia, the irrepressible no-nonsense army nurse who wore five bright bracelets on each arm, but my mom's mother, Leonore, who trembled and fluttered her hands in confusion despite her fierce intelligence.

The tightness in my father's voice was not meant to be unkind. He just didn't want us to suffer. And he was right, I didn't want to end up like Grandma Lee either, though I loved her. When she visited from Florida, she'd sit, filmy-eyed, sharp-tongued, calling everyone *darling,* brandishing her cigarette on the porch. She had been brilliant, but for the past forty years she had come in and out of making sense.

Grandma Lee's story was a patchwork not even my parents fully understood. Postpartum psychosis, a long spell in the attic of her family's brownstone, early electroshock therapy at Bellevue Hospital. An illness that no one could quite diagnose, invisible but obvious to all except her: an anxiety so intense that it could distort a life from the inside. I didn't want to be a worrywart, but I couldn't help it.

"You're a sensitive child," people told me, disapprovingly. They were right, I thought: I felt too much, worried too much. But how could I stop being who I was?

And yet, as much as I feared this mysterious power—waves that could pull me beneath the ocean and extinguish me in a second, loneliness that could do the same—I also longed to encounter it. I wanted to be tested. I studied survival guides: how to tie a knot, make a fire, which berries and leaves are edible. I longed to forage in the wild. I wanted to know what it felt like to leave everything I knew, to live on that side of a mountain alone, to find peace on the other side of fear.

∾

I was lucky, because I had an anchor in these internal storms: my violin. When I was three years old, my mother had seen a talk show about the Suzuki Method. She'd brought me to the squat cinder-block building of the local music school and rented a tiny violin with a tiny bow. As I grew older, I'd progressed from sawing "Johnny-wants-a-hot-dog" rhythms on open strings to the alchemy of music: phrasing, breath.

Now, in fifth grade, my teacher drew an *x* on the fleshy part of my fingertip with a ballpoint pen to show me where precisely to place it on the string. The pen tip tickled until it hurt; I thrilled to the feeling. The sensation of the world imprinting itself on me—and of me, in turn, learning to reflect it back out through my body, horsehair, wood, sound waves.

The mystery kept calling to me, through all the trappings of a suburban childhood. My Little Pony dolls, with long pink manes and soft plastic bodies; halogen lights in parking garages; Beethoven symphonies on the classical radio station in the car, with their hint of madness and grief. Intimate and unknowable, a dark ocean beyond the lamplight.

I felt it in the ferns, whose green leaflets and brown spores had witnessed the dinosaurs. In the stars, sending out their beacons from unknowable space. In the small violin vibrating against my left shoulder, changing the air around me. A secret at the heart of things. An untamable loneliness, the feeling of holes inside, as if I were a lotus pod, seeds rattling down deep.

Something in me rushed forward to meet the world, so fast it took my breath, knocked me down inside, although my body still stood. And sometimes, with no warning, I saw a dizzying time-lapse view of it all: cicadas, ferns uncurling, the sun rising and setting, beginnings and endings.

I thought this was all in my imagination. I didn't yet know that there was a place, a sunny second-floor room, where everyone acted as if such things were real: corners of ordinary life that explode into fireballs; prayers murmured over cups of liquid; blessings, curses, quests, survival, mountains, magic.

The Grandchildren Come Back

"We have to boil an egg!" my grandmother Sylvia wailed in grief as we prepared for my grandfather's funeral after his sudden death, and my father yelled back in his own grief, "Forget about the goddamn egg!" Somebody looked it up: *Traditionally, hard-boiled eggs are eaten at the meal of condolence which follows the death of a family member.* My mother set water to boil and my father went back to call the funeral home again.

It's an old story: my great-grandparents came to the New World and left behind the trappings of Eastern Europe. No more shtetls, no more pogroms, no more conscription into the czar's army, no more Yiddish. No more *tallit katan,* fringed ritual garments worn beneath shirts; no more leather tefillin wrapped around the forehead and left arm each morning; no more hard-boiled eggs, murmured prayers, superstitions, all bound by something powerful, a presence that touches every second of a life, *searching,* in the words of the Torah, *our kidneys and our hearts.*

Flashes of unexpected piety appeared here and there in our family, usually around deaths. But on normal days my grandparents were assimilated Jews. Freethinkers, suspicious of authority in all its forms—sentimental about their heritage, but easily disgusted by too much of it. Religious ritual was somewhere far below us, a safety net for moments of crisis. When you fell into a pit, its black mesh could hold you, keep you from plunging infinitely. But in the daylight life—work, school, meals, play, bed—we didn't need that superstitious garbage.

Still, as the Yiddish proverb says: *The children leave, and the grandchildren come back.*

∾

My sisters and I were the only Jewish kids in our public school class. Our meager observances, annual lack of Christmas tree, and olive skin stood out in the overwhelmingly Protestant, predominantly blond suburb where we lived. "What are you?" kids would ask. We knew we were different somehow, but understood little about how.

One afternoon in fourth grade, I sat outside my elementary school waiting to be picked up. I'd stayed late for some activity, so I was alone on the scratchy grass at the parking lot's entrance when a sandy-haired fifth grader on a skateboard stopped in front of me. Something in me leaped a bit. He was slight, his skater-cut flopped over his cheek. He was with a couple older kids: middle schoolers, in their majestic mystery. I couldn't believe he noticed me.

"Hey," he called out, and too late I noticed an edge in his voice. "You look Jewish. Are you Jewish? Got a nickel? Got a nipple?" And they skated off, laughing. My face burned with a new sort of shame. I never told anyone.

∾

My official religious education began at age eight, when my parents realized they had better get me started if I was going to have a bat mitzvah one day. My mother consulted the phone book; since both of my parents had grown up attending Conservative synagogues in South Florida, we ended up at the Conservative temple. Three times a week my mother drove onto the beltway and all the way to the other side of Baltimore, to the only neighborhood where Jews had been allowed to buy property a few decades ago, where most of the community still lived. After one year, we all agreed that we should be Reform Jews, who only had to go to Hebrew School once a week.

Even there, students were required to attend services on Shabbat a few times a year. On those days, my family drove across town in our green Volvo. We wore our nicest dresses, and my mother, who usually wore jeans and a mock turtleneck, twisted her lipstick up and applied it carefully, put on a gold necklace, sprayed herself with perfume.

My father parked the Volvo in the huge lot and we walked, all of us on our best behavior, past the pastel hotel-style art into the main synagogue hall, where row after row of wooden pews faced us, vast and dark brown. We found an open one toward the back and slid in, the five of us surrounded by hundreds of strangers.

The giant sanctuary was air-conditioned, impersonal. Up at the front, on the stage they called the bimah: glimpses of a jolly, regal rabbi whose belly swelled beneath his robes; a hired choir singing behind a screen, angelic and Christian-sounding in its pageantry. In the pew ahead of us, a mother brushed her long nails gently, sensually over her preteen son's shoulder, neck, and hair throughout the service. My own mother, watching this, raised her eyebrows.

The Hebrew school classrooms where we gathered each Sunday were plain. My teacher, however, had dyed red hair, long red nails, and a phone on her desk in the shape of a hot-pink flamingo. She did her best to teach the next generation about traditions she seemed to grasp loosely herself, as my peers sent paper planes flying through the air and I sat silently in the back corner.

We managed to learn the blessing for lighting candles on Friday night, *lehadlik ner shel Shabbat,* and also to learn that in the Holocaust, less than fifty years before, kids just like us were killed for being Jewish. They'd lived normal lives, going to school and playing and worrying about being popular, and then everything changed and people started to hate them. Some of them survived because neighbors hid them in attics. *Would our neighbors hide us?* I wondered, not for the last time.

But there was also the promise of a new form of magic. One day before Hebrew school, I peeked down the hallway in the opposite direction and saw a gentle glow coming from a room with a propped-open door. When I tiptoed in, I found a small side chapel with stained glass doors. It was silent, dark, and cool, and the air inside held my body gently. A current ran through me. Shivering a little, I walked down the aisle and stood before the Everlasting Light, which burned electric and red before the wooden ark holding the Torah.

From that day on, each Sunday before Hebrew school I slipped in and sat alone for a few minutes, listening to the silence. In that chapel, a sort of holiness seemed to brush up against my body like a cat. Each time I was afraid I'd imagined it, and the room would be empty—but each time I felt it there, as if it had been waiting for me.

Many years later, I found these words in a poem by Carlo Levi: *The future has an ancient heart.*

∾

I'd been raised to believe God was a faked test answer, a magician's sleight of hand, a glass floor over the Grand Canyon. As I grew older—eleven, twelve, thirteen—I secretly began to wonder: Might God be something more subtle and paradoxical, less easily dismissed? Instead of a forged signature to cover up what we could not understand, what if God were embodied by the mysteries themselves: neurons shooting across the mind's expanses; an audience of many becoming one; eons and eras of geologic time, against which our entire human species has the lifespan of a gnat?

I began to search quietly for the place where these mysteries might intersect, where all the gates would align, as in a video game: a decoder key that would unlock a sense of meaning, belonging. I wanted to find my place in the universe, my own little corner, from which everything would make sense. I hoped that key to the universe might lie out there somewhere, with the stars, or the echoes of sound waves.

I did not yet know that each of us has to build the answer ourselves.

Three Initiations

1. Blood

Cardboard boxes of tampons and pads beckoned to me from the supermarket shelves, exotic and glamorous. But I was disappointed by my still-unstained underwear every time I sat down to pee. *I'm dying to get my period,* I wrote in my diary. Bleeding would be an initiation, admitting me to an undeclared school that lay ahead: the rites of womanhood. I had not yet read the words *Lech lecha, you will leave your father's house,* but I was impatient not to be a child any longer.

As I played a video game upstairs on our family desktop computer, slouched on the wooden chair, my blue-and-green-flowered skirt from the Gap fell around my hips. I could hear my mother sautéing ground beef downstairs. Feet up on the chair, knees splayed, I touched myself over my underwear for a moment, absentmindedly. The fabric felt strange: crusty, hard. I glanced down. A pale brown stain. A lurch in my belly, like looking down from a height.

Not quite the dramatic shift I had hoped for, but still, I was relieved to be done with childhood. When I told my mom, she raised her eyebrows in surprise, nodded, and gave me a hug. The door was open now; I awaited my induction into the school of mysteries.

2. *Fire*

On the morning of the last day of eighth grade, our entire class crowded onto two school buses, wearing bathing suits under our clothes. We were on our way to the Eighth Grade Pool Party, celebrating the end of middle school.

It was a cloudy June day, and I stood at the edge of the pool wearing my brand-new jacket: aqua blue, a fancy lightweight windbreaker fabric. I had saved up for months to buy this jacket, my first clothes purchase with allowance money. It was pristine, the color of my dreams for the summer: beaches, first kisses, blonde highlights in the sun.

I heard the sound of flip-flops and chewing gum and turned to see the popular girls walking toward me. Their hair was exquisitely scrunched, their lips glossed, their skin clear. *Finally,* I thought, *they see me!* Samantha—tall, blonde, wearing gold stud earrings—stepped out in front as they approached.

"Hey, Alicia," she said sweetly. Then she gestured to the brown-haired girl beside her: "Lauren's cold. Can she borrow your jacket?"

I stammered: "I mean, uh, it's new . . ."

Samantha shook her head. "She needs it. Give it to her."

Slowly I handed over the jacket. They ran away, laughing.

Lauren came back later, wearing my jacket, a dark brown blob on the front. She unzipped the jacket and handed it to me. "Sorry about the ketchup stain," she said in a voice that actually sounded sincere. She didn't meet my eyes.

"That's a shitty thing to do, you know," said a voice behind me. I turned, holding the jacket, and saw a girl I barely knew glaring at Lauren, who was already walking away, looking embarrassed.

"They're assholes, why do you hang out with them?" the girl said to me. "Come on." She jerked her head toward a picnic table at the edge of the woods.

Far from the pool and the snack bar, the table was half-hidden by large, overgrown trees leaning toward the sun in anticipation of a Maryland summer. I shrugged. I had nowhere else to be.

"Hey," said a laconic chorus as I approached. Six kids were flopped around the table, fiddling with lighters and bottle caps.

Floppy skater haircuts, nose rings, lots of black eyeliner; I felt like I'd stepped into an alternate universe, nothing like the sunny, cannonball-diving scene at the pool, where teachers stood with arms crossed, joking with each other, and kids hurled their gleaming bodies into the water.

I'd seen these kids hanging out, always from a distance. Our school was heavily tracked, and I was in the "G-and-T" track, which my shop teacher called "garbage and trash," and the school district said was an abbreviation for "gifted and talented." None of the G-and-T kids smoked. Few even cared about things like jackets from the Gap. I felt something shift in me.

"Want a cigarette?" asked a girl with pale skin and black-painted fingernails. Half invitation, half dare. I suddenly realized why they were holding their hands beneath the table. I reflexively shook my head. And then I thought for a moment. Some calculation carried itself out in my mind, a montage:

Childhood. My love for my mother. My promise to never. The sky. Sun on the grass. Thick black eyeliner. Ketchup stain on my jacket. Distant sound of cannonballing bodies hitting the pool. Unexpected kindness. My body shimmering in the June heat. Curiosity: sharp-edged, exhilarating. The kids at the picnic table, looking at me, waiting.

It was a new feeling: not knowing my answer, forgetting my name for a moment. It felt good, that unknowing.

"Actually . . . yeah."

The girl with shiny black nails smiled. She showed me how to light it, the match so close to my face.

3. Bread

Some part of me knew that my body was average: sturdy, short, always ten pounds over the ideal weight listed in teen magazines.

Years later I would realize the privilege inherent in my average-sized shape. But I was still a child, and it was the beginning of the 1990s. "Body positivity" was not a phrase people used; Jane Fonda's self-starved figure was the feminine ideal, taut, shiny leotards and bellies flat as a rubber band. By age twelve, my revulsion at my own body was simply a part of me. It seemed impossible to escape.

Later that summer I was at the same pool, the guest of a friend whose family had a membership. We lay on our respective beach towels, chatting, and then she squinted against the sun and said, "Ugh, I feel so fat." She wasn't, but I knew she meant it; she was a serious ballet dancer. Then she sat up and leaned in, close enough that I smelled her sunscreen and bubble gum. "But guess what," she whispered. "I figured something out. There's a way to get skinny! All you have to do is . . . not eat."

I followed her lead and stayed away from the snack bar that day, the shiny crinkly packages, the Chips Ahoy and Fritos, the pizza with its orange globules of oil. It was my first lesson in renunciation.

I now know this was the beginning of a sickness, a morbid initiation. But it was also a step into my own power: the ability to separate from my own desires.

We were taught by American culture to use this power for suffering rather than for good, sickness rather than strength. Still, the capacity to choose whether or not to fulfill a desire—call it discipline, abstinence, restraint—is also a powerful spiritual practice, and that day at the pool was the first time I consciously practiced this. On Yom Kippur when I fast, I remember that initiation, though my first training in it was dangerously misguided.

When I returned to school at the end of summer, all the popular girls squealed over me. "You look so great! What did you do?"

I was beginning to learn the secret passwords: of adulthood, of power, of living in a body.

Rachel and Leah

(Book of Genesis)

In the ancient world, an older sister is supposed to marry first. But Leah has a problem with her eyes. They are tender, or weak, or soft; the translation is unclear, but we know hers is not a face that makes a person fall in love at first sight.

So when Jacob passes through their camp, he falls in love with her younger sister, Rachel, instead. Their father agrees to a wedding, on the condition that Jacob will first work for him for seven years. The story moves quickly: seven years melt into the wedding day.

But the next morning, Jacob wakes up to find that it was not his beloved Rachel beneath the veil. He has been tricked by his father-in-law into marrying Leah instead. Now he has to work another seven years for the right to marry Rachel.

In the Torah's version, both Rachel and Leah are silent pawns. Their father swaps them beneath the marriage canopy; the sisters do not speak. But in later interpretations, the ancient rabbis propose a dramatically different version of the story, adding a twist with characteristic psychological insight.

The rabbis, most of whom are fathers themselves, know how sharply children perceive their parents. Rachel and Leah's father has always been tricky; it's fair to imagine that they might suspect their father will manipulate the situation.

And the rabbis also know, often from personal experience, how those who are less powerful find ways to survive.

So, using their interpretative license—midrash, a sort of ancient Jewish fanfic tradition—the rabbis retell the story. They stay true to the contours of the plot, while adding a whole layer of narrative that gives the sisters intelligence, voice, and agency.

In this new version, when Jacob proposes, Rachel accepts. But she also warns him that her father will almost certainly try to manipulate Jacob into marrying her older sister, Leah, instead. Perhaps he'll switch them beneath the obscuring bridal veil? Jacob, who has a long history of playing tricks himself, is not concerned. He gives Rachel secret passwords, so she can prove her identity even if he can't see her face.

A brilliant plan—except that on her way to the bridal chamber, Rachel realizes that it will embarrass Leah terribly. In this moment, Rachel makes a choice to spare her sister, and betray the man she loves. She gives Leah the passwords, the wedding takes place as planned, and by the time Jacob realizes he's actually married Leah, it's too late.

This midrashic retelling, preserved in the Talmud, is one of my favorites. It's so juicy: secret passwords, sisters, a betrayal within a betrayal. When Rachel whispers the passwords to Leah, the love between sisters is more powerful than any romantic love.

Other commentaries pile on to this irresistible moment of richness in the text. One extends the deception into the marriage bed, titillatingly. It also reveals the passwords, a special treat:

> Throughout the entire wedding night Leah pretended to be Rachel, using the three passwords that Rachel had given her: *niddah* [menstruation laws], *challah,* and *lighting of candles* on Friday night, as Jacob had given them to Rachel.

Like all passwords, the words are shorthand. They stand for specific rituals: removing a small piece of challah from the loaf before baking in honor of the sacrificial bread of the ancient Temple; refraining from sexual intimacy during menstruation; and lighting candles on the eve of Shabbat and holidays.

Niddah, challah, and candle-lighting. In the world of the rabbis, this is a common grouping. These three commandments form a triad of practices considered especially sacred to women.

The idea of "women's mitzvot" can be binary, limiting, restrictive. And yet, I want to claim the power of these rituals, too. The elemental beauty. What does it mean to be a sister, a husband, a bride, a partner for life? What does it mean to live in a body? What does it mean to be a Jew?

Bread sustains us, blood flows through us, fire warms us and lights up the world. All three weave into our bodies, through our mouths and veins and eyes. *Bread, blood, fire:* fitting words to whisper during a marriage ceremony. Or, fitting words to whisper to a sister with whom you will fight for the rest of your life—because soon Rachel, too, becomes Jacob's wife.

In most weddings, two people bind themselves to each other, despite all they cannot know about each other. In this wedding, a sister gives her sister what she herself most desires, and three people braid their lives together into a new, complicated family.

Perhaps Rachel, Leah, and Jacob are unusual in this extended, intimate, impossible constellation. Or maybe they are the definition of family: complex, profound, at once disappointing and transcendent. Bound together until death by our hidden stories, our secret passwords. By fire, and bread, and blood.

Boner

In '90s suburbia, we searched for love, as teenaged humans have for tens of thousands of years—but instead of meeting at wells, we met at the mall. Boner was a sweet, quiet boy named Jake, who went by Boner because he looked like a character on a TV show I wasn't allowed to watch. He was my first boyfriend.

Boner had brown curly hair, blue eyes, and pale skin sprinkled with freckles. He lived alone with his single mom in the center house of a string of two-story row homes, perched on a hill over a six-lane road. His mother was always at work; it did not occur to me to wonder where his father was.

At fourteen, with the bravado of a child crashing through the limits of childhood, I was still determined to shed my girl-self, to be initiated into the mysteries of adulthood. Sex and drugs seemed like the obvious path.

And so it came to pass that halfway through 1991, my freshman year in high school, I decided it was time to lose my virginity and drop acid for the first time, on the same night.

"Are you sure?" Boner's forehead furrowed when I told him.

"Definitely." I nodded.

We planned a double-date sleepover in his basement with Ted

and Lisa, another high school couple. Ted was a junior and owned a beat-up car; Lisa had a beauty mark beside her lips, hazel eyes, and the world-weary air of an adult, although she was a freshman like me. Both of them somehow seemed to have access to unlimited beer. Their relationship was more like a marriage than the tentative playacting of mine with Boner; they shared a bed most nights, seemed to have no parents, and were in love.

I finished practicing my violin and headed out with my sleeping bag. I'd told my parents I was sleeping at a friend's house in our neighborhood, but instead I walked to Boner's, where Lisa was already at the kitchen table, smoking a cigarette. "Come on down," Boner called from the basement. "Ted's already here."

"I'm going to lose my virginity tonight," I whispered to Lisa as we walked downstairs. She looked at me protectively, as if she'd seen things I didn't yet know existed. I knew she probably had and was grateful for her kindness.

"Watch out for the ceiling," Boner called, and we ducked, one after the other, to avoid the beam at the bottom of the stairs.

A beige rug covered the concrete floor, a lava lamp cast a purple glow. I picked at the threads on the sofa as Ted took out a Ziploc bag with two small squares of paper. *It's just like graph paper,* I thought, and for a moment I wished I were back in chemistry class, putting on my safety goggles, rather than preparing to lose my innocence in this basement.

I closed my eyes and opened my mouth, and I felt Boner carefully place the small square of paper on my waiting tongue, a ritual sacrament. "There you go," he said kindly. The thinnest of barriers between my tongue and my soft palate. Boner opened his mouth; I lay the tiny square on his warm tongue. And then we waited.

"Prepare to have your mind blown by this movie," Ted said as he slipped a cassette into the VCR. We nestled together on the couch, breathing the musty basement air. Halfway through the movie, the stones of a wall expanded to fill the screen and began to move. They dislodged themselves, sliding around, vibrating. "Oh my god, you guys, it's working!" I said, and Boner high-fived me.

When the movie ended, he took me by the hand. We walked unsteadily, with measured, grave steps, like a newly married couple, out into the small sunken backyard. Here, against the wall in the moonlight, he dutifully embarked on my plan. We kissed, he kneaded my micro breasts in his soft hands, I unbuttoned my jeans and guided his hand into my underpants with determination and purpose. "You sure?" he asked, and I answered firmly, "Yes." He searched with his index finger and then, nervously, pushed inside me. I felt a hot dry friction, like rope burn in a place I never knew existed. "Ouch!" I blurted, and shoved him away.

Boner, horrified to have hurt me, apologized over and over. "It's okay," I whispered, hugging him. "It's okay. I'm sorry." An emptiness overtook me, spreading from my center to my edges. I'd messed up, made this gentle creature hurt me without meaning to, and now we both felt we had broken something. *There is so much I do not know about the world,* I thought, *even my own body is a mystery. I don't even know how to learn the things I want to know.*

Lisa came outside and put her arm around me. We huddled on the back basement steps, blowing twin plumes of smoke into the cold winter air, as if she were my big sister. It was a moment of pastoral care, her presence beside me on the journey.

Later that night, after hours of watching paisley patterns on the wall and tracers arcing through the sky, just as I felt myself beginning to return to the ordinary world, I noticed a small mirror sitting on the basement table. I looked into it and saw my own brown eyes looking back at me from the face of an old woman. Peering closer, I saw that she was not just any old woman—she was me, in the future. She had a crown of white hair, and a net of wrinkles across her tan face, and she smiled at me compassionately. *I'm waiting for you,* I felt her say. Her presence was like Lisa's: comforting, patient, wiser than I was. She could hold all my embarrassment and shame, every last liquid-hot drop, and still beam with love for my human-ness as she waited patiently, my crone-self, for me to grow into her.

∾

I'm not yet that silver-haired woman who smiled at my teenage self in the mirror. But I'm closer to her, now, than to my young self. I take my place in the mirror and look out at those young eyes—the eyes of myself in the past, the eyes of my students now. I see a longing for ancestral wisdom that feels impossible to reach in a world of strip malls and screens and plastic bags. You will learn, I want to tell that girl. You will learn to walk its ancient labyrinth step by step. And then you will learn to step out of those lines, into the uncharted desert of your own heart.

Judith

One moment Judith is a young widow wearing sackcloth and ashes in a city under siege. The next, she is a warrior disguised in her finest clothes, walking directly into the enemy camp at midnight. She transforms so quickly, it's as if her warrior-self had been hiding inside her for a long time, waiting for the right moment to emerge.

The men in power have declared that military defeat is inevitable, but Judith (and her maid, Abra) choose action over despair. Their willingness to risk everything leads to the famous scene, dramatic enough to earn countless depictions in Old Masters paintings, operas, and ballets: these two women befriend the enemy general Holofernes, ply him with cheese and wine, then cut his head off with his own sword.

Judith and Abra are unlikely war heroes with an unexpectedly grisly strategy. It's compassionate, too, maintaining a surgical economy of violence: in killing the general, they save countless innocent lives. This victory defies the predictions of all the military and religious experts of her town, not to mention the expectations of young women in the ancient world—or ours, for that matter.

The book of Judith is apocryphal in Judaism, meaning the ancient rabbis did not include it in the official canon of the Hebrew Bible. But many Jewish communities—in particular, Jewish women—have claimed Judith's story as part of their living tradition. Because elements of her saga echo the Chanukah story, Judith is associated with that holiday, and rituals honoring her have been performed by Jewish women on Chanukah throughout the centuries, from North Africa to Eastern Europe to Turkey. A tiny sculpture of Judith holding a sword (and sometimes Holofernes's head) adorns the top of many historic Chanukah menorahs.

Judith's is a story of resistance, hope, and transformation. Challenging the city's leaders, who accept their impending defeat as God's will, Judith takes matters into her own hands. From her position of grief and seemingly powerlessness, she arises, directly contradicts the men in power—and saves her people. She is God's instrument in the world.

What gives Judith the courage to sneak out under cover of darkness and walk directly into the enemy general's tent? What gives her the courage to defy the men in power?

Judith is a young woman, and her story carries a tinge of late adolescence. The maidservant who watches her; the beautiful dresses she slips into; her easy seduction of the general; the lack of responsibilities that allow her to mourn for three years after her husband dies, without needing to rouse herself and care for anyone else. Perhaps this connection to the fierce visions of late adolescence supports Judith in her willingness to challenge the men in power, to risk everything—including her life—as she unfurls, revealing the warrior inside.

Fasting, Recreational Drugs, and Other Practices of the Early Suburban Ascetics

I can't believe you don't know the Winterland bootleg," Tim said as he passed me the joint. We were cutting fifth period to drink sodas—Mountain Dew for him, Diet Pepsi for me—behind the arbor vitae hedge of the small office park across from our school. "That fucking solo on 'Cream Puff War.' And you call yourself a Deadhead."

At fourteen, almost done with ninth grade, I did call myself a Deadhead, although Tim was right: for me it was more about the scene than the music. I stopped curling my bangs and instead braided a strand of my hair, threaded through with embroidery floss and skull-shaped beads. I wore oversized batik dresses and dabbed rose oil on my wrists and let my armpit hair grow. I burned small black cones of incense—partially for forensic reasons, to cover the smell of cigarettes, and partially because it calmed me to watch the smoke perform its gymnastic ascent toward the sky.

I was beginning to sense a world of adventure outside my suburban public high school. Inside its cinder-block walls, conformity ruled; we spent our days surrounded by fluorescent lights, concrete floors, and attendance sheets, and standing out in any way was viewed with suspicion.

At a Dead show, though, life force was everywhere. Before every show, the gray expanse of parking lot outside would transform into an open-air festival, desolate concrete filling with color: bead makers and jewelry makers and leatherworkers and musicians and meditators and tarot readers and massage therapists and people dancing barefoot on the asphalt. In that world, dread locked twentysomethings handed out peanut butter and jelly sandwiches to strangers; patchouli-drenched seekers wandered across the country in VW vans, picking up new friends along the way. It was a space of communal highs, of magic and possibility; the opposite of high school.

And so, each time the Grateful Dead toured within an hour of Baltimore, I figured out a way to go, which involved complicated fabrications for the benefit of my parents. "Don't worry, my friend Sara's aunt is driving us and she'll be with us the whole time," I would say. "Well, I guess that's all right," said my mother, unaware that Sara's aunt was nineteen years old and a committed stoner.

Sara was a senior and, like her aunt, a real Deadhead. She was a gorgeous, sunny blonde who looked more California than Baltimore. She could have been a popular girl, a cheerleader, a field hockey player—but instead she wore her hair long and straight and smoked pot and had a hazy smile that seemed, to me, as wise as a goddess. In my dreams, I, too, would be cheerleader material who chose to go deep with the Grateful Dead. Instead, I was a short, acne-ridden kid.

But in the parking lot, people saw beyond my disappointing exterior. I felt not only the absence of judgment, but the presence of love. No one cared how anyone smelled or whether they'd brushed their hair; strangers looked strangers in the eyes and smiled. Ticket-less, I wandered around the parking lot with my science lab book held out in front of me, *Looking for a miracle* written in curlicue letters on the light blue grid. Someone always had an extra ticket, usually for free: a miracle.

Inside the stadium, I stood in line for the bathroom, the sounds of the band echoing off the cavernous concrete. A gorgeous twenty-year-old guy with tan skin and a long blond ponytail walked up and handed me a single daffodil. "A pretty flower for a pretty girl," he said, and walked away.

I wanted that moment to be a part of me forever. I bit the daffodil off its stem, chewing, taking the moment inside me with each bitter yellow crunch.

∾

A few months later, time slowed and expanded as my friend Mandy and I stood beside York Road, the six-lane thoroughfare of our suburb, waiting to cross the street. The cars sped by in both directions, impossibly quickly, as if we were standing next to a racetrack. But we weren't, of course; it was the same road I took to get to school every day. I turned and said to Mandy, "Time is moving faster on the other side." We repeated it together like a chant: "Time is moving faster on the other side."

Leave your father's house, God said to Abraham, and though I still did not know the words, by now I definitely heard the call. Abraham walked out the door that day. My situation was a little different; I would be living in my parents' house for three more years. I wasn't ready to leave, and I didn't feel any particular joy in disobeying my parents. But I was committed to going deeper into the experience of being human, by any means necessary, and the necessary means happened to be forbidden.

And so I left my parents' house without leaving. I was a disciple and LSD was my monastery, my teacher, and my instruction. It was a hidden door, a mystery rabbit hole, an ascetic practice to be hidden from my parents and, of course, my two younger sisters.

My covert journeys kept me up all night, sitting in my bedroom, ears painfully over-attuned to any noise as I tried to keep from waking my parents. I wrote in my journal, stared at patterns on the walls, received holograms of wisdom that passed through me one after another like waves. At two in the morning, I crept to the bathroom to watch my face transform in the mirror, by now a comforting sight I could command at will. fast-forwarding to my thirties, my fifties, my eighties, and then rewinding back to my fourteen-year-old face, and still further, until I had the face I remember seeing in the mirror as a young girl, and then as a baby.

On those long nights I learned self-reliance. Sometimes panic would well up, a pure anxiety thrumming through my net of nerves. I had to learn to calm myself: to distract myself with counting, to write down each experience until it began to dissolve in the light of my own mind. To stretch, to bargain, to pray to unseen powers. *Keep me safe. Watch over me.*

Over and over, the experience of giving birth to myself: it hurt, it was a miracle, I wanted it to end. When I emerged in the morning, I was a warrior, drinking tea at my parents' kitchen table with my secret.

Many years later, I would come to understand that these nights were another initiation. The teachings I would devour from the holy books describe the same structures I first glimpsed during those long nights alone in my childhood bedroom—not yet an adult, but no longer a child.

My Grandfather Rewrites Genesis

One day I would travel far in search of the sacred. But for now I was looking for it in suburban Maryland. And since there is holiness everywhere, even the high school had its sacred corners: the loading dock hidden in the crook of the parking lot, where student smokers hid; the tucked-away strip of grass behind the football field; the orchestra room with its patina of decades of spit on the reed and brass instruments, decades of finger-skin cells on the violin necks.

Most sacred of all was the art room, and its high priestess was Mrs. O'Brien, the art teacher, a stunning woman in her late forties. She carried herself with the grace of a celebrity, painted her face like a movie star, and wrapped herself in colorful scarves. A glorious combination, she was both den mother and aesthete, a world traveler and connoisseur of finer things with an intensely personal interest in the dramas of her students' lives.

Mrs. O'Brien let us hide in her room when we cut chemistry class. She gave us copies of Kandinsky's manifesto, *Concerning the Spiritual in Art*. She pretended not to notice when we made out with each other on the mustard-colored couch behind the wall where gessoed canvases hung drying, where I first kissed a girl, a redheaded photographer named Phoebe. She encouraged us to drink coffee from her Mr. Coffee drip machine, and she let us stir in heaping spoonfuls of the powdered flavored creamer that seemed to me the ultimate in sophistication: cappuccino, amaretto, Irish Cream.

Art and coffee, beauty and the tantalizing edges of adulthood beginning to come clear. What did it mean to be an artist in a woman's body? Mrs. O'Brien and I stood side by side in her coffee corner, scraping powdered creamer from a tin with plastic spoons, when she suddenly turned to me and sighed: "I should really drink my coffee black, I'm getting fat." Glamorous, beautiful Mrs. O'Brien, whose ex-husband was a rich asshole and had left her the house, who spent summers in Italy and had a lover there, whose legs were extraordinary. "Me too," I said, and I meant it; I'd gained ten pounds, unwillingly, losing the tug-of-war between my appetite for food and my appetite for visible bones. "No," Mrs. O'Brien said, shaking her head firmly. "You're becoming a woman. And I'm becoming my mother."

∾

Art was a cultural inheritance in my family, too, although it had faded into the past since my Grandpa Dick died.

He and Grandma Lee were teenage sweethearts when he courted her by mail from Washington Heights, in Upper Manhattan, a world away from her Brooklyn home. In the Heights, Grandpa Dick grew up with Leonard Bernstein and Adolph Green and a whole crop of ultra-creative first-generation Jewish immigrant boys who went on to change the artistic landscape of America.

Dick's envelopes to Lee were elaborately illustrated pieces of art. Around Lee's carefully inked address, an entire world unfolds. In summer, when she was visiting relatives in Massachusetts, her address is written across a barn; behind it, a bucolic country scene stretches to the edges of the envelope, with sheep, fences, a dozing farmer. Back in Brooklyn the next fall, Dick draws a man reading a newspaper on the subway; one side of the paper is filled by Lee's address on St. Mark's Place, the other with squiggles standing in for headlines, a cartoon of Hitler reading a Yiddish newspaper, surrounded by floating swastikas. Postmark: 1939.

Family legend holds that the mailman eagerly awaited Dick's envelopes and was more disappointed than Lee when he didn't write.

Grandpa Dick, aka Dick Briefer, aka Dick Hamilton, grew up to create the Frankenstein comics during the glory days of that industry. He wrote and illustrated the entire series. A few years after Grandma Lee recovered from her first mental breakdown, they moved to Florida, where, despite the odds, he supported the family as a comic artist.

And then one day, the fashions changed. Or maybe, as some family members suspect, he was unofficially blacklisted for drawing the "Pinky Rankin" comic in the Communist paper *The Daily Worker.* Either way, he ended up supporting my mother's family, barely, by drawing pastel caricatures. He set up his easel at the local mall, he traveled to fraternity houses and sketched college kids at parties. Though he died when I was three, the image of his beautiful hand sketching some drunk frat boy's portrait makes my artist-heart hurt a little for him.

Art, magic, love; what constellation do these dots form? The ability to create a world with a piece of paper and pen, to delight even the mailman as a teenager; the inability to take away the suffering of the person you love most.

Maybe every artist is, in their own way, an outsider. Maybe a person has to see life from a distance in order to interpret it. Maybe that distance, too, can be handed down over the generations. Perhaps that is why, over time, that sense of a gap between me and the world, which had troubled me so deeply as a child, began to transform into a gift, a space into which to create.

∾

I suspect that Grandma Lee should have been a writer, though to my knowledge she did not write. She loved literature and had majored in English at Brooklyn College in the 1930s. In her nursing home bed decades later, she could still recite the prologue to *The Canterbury Tales,* long after she could distinguish her granddaughters, though in fairness I suppose we must have blurred—three dark-haired, violin-playing teenagers, Manic Panic tinting our bangs magenta or forest green or electric blue.

We were all color, with our rainbow hair, our rainbow tights, our blue and red flannels. Grandma Lee was pale, almost translucent. Milky-eyed, her hair the white of milk, she turned her head to look at me mischievously, licked her lips dramatically, and in a clear voice she recited:

Whan that Aprille with his shoures soote,
The droghte of March hath perced to the roote,
And bathed every veyne in swich licóur
Of which vertú engendred is the flour.

Once, years later, I visited Grandma Lee in the nursing home near my parents' house. "Hi, Grandma," I said brightly from the doorway, and she responded, "Oh, hello! You haven't gotten fat, that's good!" I sat beside the bed holding her hand, the texture of a lily, as she said to me with venom in her voice, "Your grandfather should be *ashamed* of himself. He had himself *exhumed* to have an affair with that woman."

And yet she and Grandpa Dick stayed married for fifty years, despite her delusions (which began in her late twenties, receded, then came and went over decades). They stayed married despite the paintings that show the hours my grandfather spent in his studio with a nude model (could this be the woman she still envied, so many years later?). And it seems he loved my grandmother, too; he never stopped making art for her, beginning with the envelopes he decorated as a teenager, and culminating in the fifteen-page fully illustrated love letter he gave her for her sixtieth birthday, a few years before he died.

The letter is breathtaking—an illuminated manuscript. On thick white cardstock bound with black leather, my grandfather rewrites Genesis. God creates the world, but is not satisfied; animals appear, then humans, but it's not enough. God creates Beethoven, and is pleased, but knows something to be missing. And then, finally, God creates Leonore—my Grandma Lee—and at last the world is complete. The final page is a portrait of her face, radiant, elegant, her high cheekbones shining, her eyes glowing with joy.

When he was drawing, my grandfather was God, and God was an artist, and together they created my grandmother, and all her imperfections became luminous.

I wonder: What would Grandma Lee have created? If she were God, and God were an artist—what story would they have written together?

To Be an Instrument

Nobody made me practice for three hours a day at music camp; I wanted to. I loved my practice room, a wood-paneled classroom beneath the library, with trees surrounding me on all sides. Suburbia was a world away, with its gas stations and malls, its polished high school floors; here the summer was unbearably green, the light beneficent, my fellow campers as odd and geeky as I was. At morning circle, we sat with our teachers in silence for a full minute, breathing together. At sunset, we lay in the scratchy grass of the Upper Field's far reaches, whispering secrets. All through the hot afternoons the sound of practicing echoed along the hallways: bassoon and piano, flute and cello, scales, phrases, repetition, weaving ribbons through the July air.

Looking back, I see how spiritual practice hides inside what we call secular life. After each practice session, I returned my violin carefully to its blue satin bed, wiping the rosin off the tea-colored wood, zipping up the black rectangular case, and returning it to its spot of honor beside my bed. Then I jogged three miles in the ninety-five-degree heat, always trying to outrun my lunch, returning just in time to shower and slip into my place in the chorus, singing Mozart's high, clear notes from *The Magic Flute:*

Three spirits young and wise will guide you, and on your journey stay beside you.

I practiced as I had been taught, slowly and with focus, repeating each phrase again and again. I worked on making my bow changes imperceptible, so that if you listened with closed eyes, you could not identify the moment when an up-bow became a down-bow, my elbow loosely guiding the long thin wood-and-horsehair along the string. I practiced my intonation, half my mind resting on the sunlit leaves outside the window and the other half inside the finger I placed on the A-string, carefully, finding the precise home where the note rang true. *Rely on them where they may lead, only their counsel shall you heed.*

I was teaching my body to find the place that resonates, the place of beauty, where overtones align. When I found that place, I felt the notes vibrate through my jaw, my skull, the shimmering air around me. When I found that place, my violin played me, music emanating from the bones of my face. That was what I wanted, like any worshipper: to be an instrument.

∾

Back home in fall, I followed my new school friends to another world of music: ear-searing, next-day-buzzing, skull-tingling, church-basement rock shows. I tore black tights to spiderweb shreds, pulled a blue ski cap over my forest-green hair (Manic Panic!), and threw myself into the mosh pit, flailing wildly to the music. Some bands were casually formed in my own high school; others were older, more serious bands in their early twenties, who drove up from D.C. or down from Philly or in from the farther-out exurbs of Baltimore. The shows themselves were the centerpiece of our weekends: like fucked-up debutante balls for the weirdos, where we paraded our eyeliner, how casually we held our cigarettes, how loud we laughed with our friends.

Here, again, the particular kindness of those who did not fit in: sweaty, tattooed, rainbow-haired weirdos who looked out for everyone who entered the circle, protecting each other even as they hurled their bodies together. I lost myself in the mass of bodies writhing to the music, just as hours had disappeared in the honeyed light of the practice room alone with my violin.

Shows were organized by the bands themselves, and held in whatever spaces could be convinced to host a couple hundred teenagers on a weekend night. We went wherever the xeroxed flyers told us to go, and since Towson was full of churches, with basements and social halls available for cheap, we often found ourselves in their dark, chilly spaces on Saturday nights. And it was indeed a form of worship—bands at the center, the scene surrounding them, the ecstasy of being together unsupervised. On show nights, hordes of us would descend on the venue, dropped off by parents or pulling into the church lot in borrowed station wagons. We filed in one by one, each handing five dollars to a kid with a cash box at the door, who in return drew a wide permanent-marker X on the backs of our hands with permanent marker as proof we'd paid.

Inside, pure teenaged life-energy seethed along with the music. Some of us were straightedge, abstaining from drugs and alcohol as a matter of principle; others smuggled vodka in water bottles, passed joints around in the parking lot, and popped Vivarin pills to power our dancing. I could go either way. Between bands, the front doors propped open, we poured out onto the concrete with the steamy air. When I was lucky, I'd find a cute boy to talk to, standing side by side with our backs against the brick church wall, both of us staring out at the mass of smoking kids, the street-lit trees. "Are you into the Piltdown Men?" one of us would ask, and the other would say, "Oh, yeah, *Tipper Gore Shoots Smack* is the most amazing album." If I was really lucky, we'd kiss, and the world around us would briefly disappear.

~

I wasn't brave enough to kiss girls in public, though, and I wasn't alone. In early '90s suburbia, queerness was barely recognized and certainly not celebrated. This was the era of "Don't Ask, Don't Tell"; the military would stop kicking out its gay members, but only if they agreed to hide their identities and relationships. Like the subtle racism that pervaded every element of our lives but went largely unnoticed by white communities, homophobia was a thrumming bass line—so consistent it was taken for granted. In fact, the general vibe of liberals in our suburb was self-congratulatory; how far we'd come as a society, accepting that people shouldn't be fired or shunned for their private sexuality! Queerness in public, though, was out of bounds.

Even at my music camp, where many of the male teachers had "friends" who would come visit each summer, queerness had to be spoken of in code. It would be a decade until these "friends" could be publicly called "partners," and another two before they could be legally declared "husbands" or "spouses." Back in my suburban high school, longing beat beneath the surface, and things happened in the dark (even between teachers). But there was no Gay-Straight Alliance, no question that straightness was normal and queerness deviant; not once in my twelve years of public school did I have an openly queer teacher.

And me? I had always known I liked both boys and girls, since before I knew there was a name for it. As a child, I'd snuck forbidden TV one afternoon while my parents were out, and watched in horror as Oprah interviewed a teenaged boy who had been disowned by his parents for coming out as gay. I ran upstairs sobbing and hid in my bedroom, refusing to emerge, crying so hard the snot covered my face and hands. Later that evening my mother knelt outside the door patiently, asking every few minutes for me to let her in, to tell her what was wrong. Finally, I opened the door and out it poured, hot and frightening like vomit: "Would you still love me if I were gay?" Yes, she assured me, she would.

Though this was a tremendous relief, and I know how lucky I am to have received that answer, that boy's story lodged itself in my child-mind, a cautionary tale: a whiff of danger, of being hated and shunned for who I was inside. I knew I wasn't gay the way he was, but I knew I wasn't not-gay, either. I stuffed the question away, filing it in the deep, dark folder of things not to think about.

And now here I was: fourteen years old and determined to live authentically. In this context, my sexuality—I was learning to call it "bi," a satisfying one-syllable name for something complex and indescribable—was going to have to be okay, if not with those around me, then at least with me. I'd never ever met an adult who publicly identified as bi, and I wasn't sure what it meant to live that sort of a life, but I was trying to figure it out.

Each person I touched was a new country, with their own language, tastes, and smells, their own expectations and customs. We were not "together," we were something else: partners in a tenuously casual square dance, young students in the school of love, making the rounds and trying not to get too attached.

Still, shame—absorbed from the culture around me and reinforced by the slurs casually tossed around—was interwoven with my defiant self-acceptance. And so I kissed boys against the brick church wall and kept my hookups with girls quiet.

∾

Along with exploration and the quest for self-acceptance was a devotion to renunciation, which I could not leave behind. I was not drawn to death, but I was drawn to beauty. That's why I practiced scales over and over, reaching for precision; that's why I threw myself into the mosh pit, flinging myself after abandon; and why I touched the cheeks of my gorgeous friends with such wonder after we kissed.

When it came to my own body, though, I'd been so deeply trained to think of beauty as thinness, thinness beauty, that I conflated it with truth, like some fucked-up romantic poet. Even beautiful Mrs. O'Brien in the art room bemoaned her beautiful hips, *tsk*ing at her own indulgence for adding the cappuccino-flavored creamer to her coffee.

And there was something else, too, that drew me deeper into the attempt to resist food. It felt like the first spiritual quest I'd encountered, an elemental challenge: entering the cave of my own desires and overcoming myself.

I developed a new interest in the Catholic saints. I looked up to them as athletes of the spirit, and fasting was the arena in which they demonstrated their inner strength. What better practice of renunciation than to resist one's most basic biological impulse? What better laboratory to explore the boundary between body and soul? They not only understood my desire to overcome the flesh, they lived it: embracing suffering, mastering their carnal desires, moving on to a higher form of love. Saint Thérèse of Lisieux: *You cannot be half a saint; you must be a whole saint or no saint at all.*

But there I was, not even half a saint. Though I tried, I wasn't good at starving myself. I had brief periods of real thinness, but there was a threshold I couldn't cross; at a certain point, my physical instincts would take over and feed me, as if I were possessed.

Now, of course, I am grateful for this inability to walk toward death. Rather than learn from the saints, I follow the wisdom of the poet Eve Ewing: *I learned that everything about me could be round and full if I let it.* Learning to love this body is a more sacred, and ultimately more difficult, practice than trying to polish it down to bone. But at the time I couldn't stop trying, and failing, to transcend the physical shape I'd been born into.

And then Tracey died.

I didn't know her well—she was a grade ahead of me—but everyone knew who she was. She had been a lacrosse star, with pale skin, light freckles, her blonde hair pulled back from her face in a ponytail. But then she became gaunt and gray. Her eyes sank behind her sharpened cheekbones, her hands were a jumble of tendons. Tracey had been to rehab, and returned a grade behind, to my classroom. She kept ten jelly beans on a tissue on her desk and ate them at regular intervals throughout the class. She was there, but not there; we could see she was being sucked under, pulled to another place. Death shone through her eyes.

One day, Tracey stopped coming to school, and soon the news of her funeral was whispered across the homeroom table. I noticed the pool of silence that covered her absence in the school: no words of acknowledgment during morning announcements in the classrooms where she had spent her days. She just slipped away, age sixteen.

I had distinguished my battle from hers. Tracey's struggle was a disease, I told myself; I was just striving for discipline, looking for beauty, testing the edge between desire and will. But after her death, I could not attempt to starve myself anymore. It took me a while to let go of the conviction that bones were beautiful and flesh repulsive, but I saw all too clearly where this quest led: the empty space where Tracey used to sit in health class, on an ugly industrial high school chair, ten jelly beans spread out on a white square of tissue.

She taught me what the Lives of the Saints could not: perfection may be beautiful to pursue, but it is deadly to hold. In October of eleventh grade, I lost my faith, that particular, punishing strain. Or maybe I just decided to leave it. *I will walk into the autumn sun,* I thought. *I will live in the body I have been given. I will eat lunch.*

∾

Steps led from the end of my street down a steep hill to a cul-de-sac; we called them the Magic Steps. Formed from railroad ties laid horizontally, the steps wound through a miniature forest of ivy and maple, the hillside's overgrown slope. Here I would hide, smoke cigarettes, and fill an endless succession of notebooks: the water-stained fat turquoise one, the flat wide-ruled red one, the paisley one with the puffy cover.

In the thick of a humid Maryland summer, nursing a cigarette on the Magic Steps, with purple nail polish on my fingernails and a symphony of cicadas in the trees, I read *A Portrait of the Artist as a Young Man.* Stephen Dedalus fell in love with God, with self-denial, and I vibrated along with every word. Then I followed him as he began to let go of asceticism and awaken to beauty.

I read *The Prophet, Siddhartha,* Mary Oliver. I read a small black book called *Japanese Death Poems,* written in the final moments of each poet's life:

I cast the brush aside—
from here on I'll speak to the moon
face to face.

So I wasn't the only one who couldn't stop wondering what it meant to live in a body that would die, who yearned to live in relationship with the mystery hidden beneath the everyday, to speak to the moon face-to-face. This longing wasn't exactly forbidden in the cinder blocks of high school, but except for the art room, it wasn't really spoken of, either. And yet it lived inside all of us. I felt the sky open a bit, seeing it for the first time. *Round and full.*

Wise-Hearted Women

(Book of Exodus)

The Mishkan, often translated as "Tabernacle," is a portable Temple that God instructs the Israelites to build after the Exodus from Egypt; they will carry it with them throughout the desert. At each new campsite, they will assemble this sacred tent as a meeting place between Divine and human. Mishkan literally means "dwelling place," and some see in this structure a parallel to the body, a temporary dwelling place we carry with us wherever we go, and perhaps the essential meeting site for Divine and human.

In the language of the Torah, notably, women are explicitly invited to build this dwelling place alongside the men. In our contemporary language, I would translate this to include all genders. The language God uses for the people who will collaborate on this sacred art-and-architecture project is *chacham-lev,* which literally means "wise-hearted." Those with skill in building, crafts, decoration, creativity—all are invited to come forward and collaborate to create this magical, liminal space.

Beautiful as this idea is, it raises some questions. Why does an omnipotent God, who created the entire world and everything in it, need a dwelling place in this world? And why does God ask *us* to build that home?

Perhaps this is a hint of Divine vulnerability—a break from the somewhat exhausting concept of Divine omnipotence. Or maybe the point is not to house God after all, but to support the Israelites in a moment of profound transition. After centuries of enslavement in Egypt, perhaps they need a physical structure to help them focus their energies on the Ineffable. Or maybe constructing the Mishkan is a team-building activity, like the ropes course at the beginning of summer camp.

Or could this passage instead gesture toward the impossibly complex, multidirectional relationship between humans and the Divine—how we need each other equally?

After all, the world would go on without humans. There would still be floods, stars, the red edge of the universe. But God, in the particular version experienced through the human heart—would that specific manifestation of divinity exist without humans making space for it?

The words of this biblical passage are thousands of years old. The Ark has been lost, the Mishkan is long gone, and the passage itself, with its instructions about weaving and construction and how to properly assemble the wooden support beams, can be hard to connect to. In fact, this section is not infrequently compared to a furniture assembly pamphlet.

But when we look past its literal details to the broader shape of this passage, this story shines. It's about the sanctity of creativity and craft, the meaningfulness of making, and the possibility of weaving sacredness out of the everyday. When we use our talents, skills, hands, and wise hearts to create beauty in any form, we perform a holy act. We invite God in.

Perhaps this is why artistic inspiration is often seen as Divine. And though our society likes to distinguish between art and craft—seeing great poets as Divinely inspired, and great quilters as merely "skilled"—this passage teaches us that Divinity is honored anytime humans create beauty, whether it's a circle of river stones arranged just so by a child or marble carved into a human form.

Through our bodies we create beauty. Through our bodies we invite the sacred into our world. And in a world that trains us to consider our physical forms in a harsh light, maybe part of our wise-hearted work is learning to see our bodies' beauty, to honor our most intimate temples.

Sliding Glass Doors, Sex, and Other Sacred Things

September 1994. Goodbye Maryland, hello Manhattan! I lay on my thin mattress and listened to an orchestra of car alarms, chirping and blaring in an endless cycle. To me, they were glamorous, a Morse code narration of New York City.

The glamour was dimmed only slightly by the fact that I lived in a freshman dorm, a giant brick tower on upper Broadway. Concrete, elevators, security turnstiles, industrial vinyl flooring: my dorm could not have been more different from the house I'd grown up in. I was two hundred miles away from the pink carpet on the stairs, the wood grain on the banister, the squeak of the hot-water faucet in the bathroom of my parents' house.

Living with two strangers in a tiny dorm room in the exhilarating and uncaring city, I held on tight to what I knew about myself. My violin was an anchor, the familiar feel of my fingers curling around the case's black handle as I crossed Broadway to audition for the university orchestra.

And something else began to call to me, too, another part of myself: my Jewishness. For the first time, I lived within walking distance of a synagogue—multiple synagogues, in fact, made of brick or stone, with Hebrew letters I couldn't decipher arching over the doorways. I was in classes with people who wore Jewish stars around their necks. In this light, my own Jewishness became more visible to me, like a thread that had passed through each of my ancestors and now ran through me. I felt aware for the first time of being a bead on this thread.

But what does a bead on a thread *do*? I'd learned a few things in Hebrew school: *hamotzi lechem min ha'aretz, borei p'ri hagafen*. The bread blessing, the wine blessing. I wanted to recite them but wouldn't have known how to explain what I was doing; these observances felt private, almost forbidden. So I waited for my roommates to leave on Friday nights, then held my own makeshift Shabbat ritual alone, with whatever I had on hand. I whispered the challah blessing over potato chips, the wine blessing over a bottle of Budweiser.

~

That fall, I began to notice the girls in long skirts. Not always, but sometimes, they stood waiting by the entrance to our dorm's sliding glass doors. When my body triggered the doors open, they would follow me in. Who *were* they? What were they doing lingering by the doors? I, too, hung around on sidewalks, but only to finish my cigarettes, and they didn't look like the type to smoke.

It took me until winter to finally approach one of the girls. Wearing a long denim skirt and a maroon puffy coat, she stood just beyond range of the door's automatic sensors on a freezing February afternoon. "Uh, excuse me," I said. "Sorry if this is a weird question, but . . . why are you waiting for someone else to make the door open?"

She tugged her coat around her and looked at me, wary and proud. "Oh, I'm Jewish," she said.

This explained exactly nothing; I shrugged. "Me too."

"Oh." Her brow furrowed. "Well . . . I'm Orthodox, and we don't use electricity on the Sabbath. So we have to wait until someone else walks in."

With these words, something deep in my brain began to blink itself awake, some primal but wise place, like a buried jewel being called to life. An awareness of the sacred in everything.

This shimmering feeling had surfaced over and over throughout my life. I felt it as I watched the punks hold out their arms to protect each other from falling in the mosh pit, in ecstatic exploration of a bright yellow daffodil at a Dead show, and in the vibrations my bow drew from the body of my violin, coloring the air around me, tying me to the bodies of everyone listening.

But I had no idea that holiness could be *in a door.* This ugly, institutional, massive pane of glass, which led to the lobby of our dorm where I'd show my ID to the guard and walk through the turnstile to the double room I shared with two other people because of a housing shortage on campus—this *door* was connected to God?

Later I would learn that this sort of thing annoyed secular, science-minded Jews (like my father) immensely. The complaint goes something like this: Why would a law against lighting a fire on the Sabbath three thousand years ago mean you shouldn't use electricity on the Sabbath today? And why would a modern person feel bound by that prohibition? And if it's so wrong to use electric sliding glass doors, why would someone else walking in first make it okay for you to walk in? And finally, why the hell would God care?

But I was thrilled. It made sense to me; something clicked into place, a mysteriously shaped hole that had been waiting for its puzzle piece, complete at last.

I'd long had the sense that everything in the world, even the simplest object, could be sacred, although it would be strange to speak about this. The hole in the hedge where I used to hide and smoke with my high school friends; the little stone hut in the woods behind the college where I'd gather sticks, hold a match to the kindling till it caught fire, and write in my journal by its light. Fire, and objects, and time, and the ballet of our bodies moving through space; automatic sliding doors, and Saturdays—*They do matter!* I thought. *They are sacred. It's not just me.*

Standing beside the girl in the denim skirt, watching her wait for someone else to walk through the doors first, I looked around at the world, and the world looked back at me, lit up with possibility.

Nearer, My God, to Thee

A sunny March day in 1997, my next-to-last spring of college: more of it behind me than ahead.

On one of those sudden spring afternoons when everything blooms at once in New York, I was hurrying back uptown to my dorm. I'd almost reached the subway stairs at Union Square when I heard the most extraordinary sound—somewhere between a party, a demolition derby, and a thousand birds flapping their wings at once.

I looked up to see a tall guy in a newsboy cap sawing away at a violin. He looked like a giant, overgrown sprite, and he was playing like no one I had ever seen. For all my years of lessons, I had no idea how he was getting those sounds out of his instrument. I forgot about my rush to get home, the cacophony of taxis and kids yelling faded into the background. All I could hear was the music: a woven interplay of Baroque gentility and screeching raucousness.

The fiddler saw me watching. He raised his eyebrows and bowed to me slightly without skipping a beat, his bow arm still cutting through the air madly. When the song ended, I put a dollar in his case. He stretched and nodded in thanks. "Hey," I said, "uh, that sounds amazing. I play too, but . . . not like that."

"Well, thank you," he said. "In fact, I'm just about ending my shift. Buy me a pint of Guinness and I'll teach you a tune?"

The bar was dark and empty, and we had our choice of booths at the back. I sipped the bitter, velvety foam off my pint as Thomas explained the music to me. "Those Appalachian tunes are a hybrid. Half of it's African rhythms brought over on the ships with enslaved people. The other half are English and Irish melodies that came over with white settlers."

Fiddle, Thomas explained, was the same instrument as violin, just played differently. "Sometimes the bridge is carved more flat on a fiddle," he said, lifting his violin case up onto his lap, "but really there's no difference except the technique." He unsnapped the case and took out his fiddle, his large hands gentle. I thought he'd demonstrate, but instead he held the instrument out to me. "Here," he said, "you try."

Before I put the bow to the strings, Thomas was already correcting me. "Naw, hold it down in front of you, not up high like a classical player. Okay, good, good. Now move your hand a couple inches up the bow, so you can really saw with your bow arm. That's more like it." The technique was atrocious from a classical perspective, but then again, I suddenly realized how uptight classical technique looked from an old-time perspective. All these ways of playing the same instrument. All these ways of living on the same planet.

"And another thing," Thomas said. "Old-time music makes people really, really happy. All sorts of people."

Over the next few weeks, in exchange for a steady string of pints, Thomas taught me to play old-time fiddle. It felt like the magic of learning a new language, like hearing my own mouth form unfamiliar words. I forced my left hand to stop the vibrato my teachers had so carefully trained me to perfect. My bow arm relaxed, my elbows drooped, shoulders slumped, my right foot began to stomp in time with the beat. The movement ricocheted up to the crown of my head, my whole torso rocking back and forth with the rhythm. "My violin teachers would be horrified," I said, shaking my head.

"Yeah," Thomas replied, grinning, "you're doing great! In fact, you're ready for some busking." He winked. "Twin fiddles make good money."

We opened our cases next to the subway entrance at Union Square during rush hour, when a stream of commuters was guaranteed to walk past us. Thomas taught me to start with three dollars in my case—"If it's empty, they won't put anything in, no matter how good you are." That day, I became a part-time street musician. For the next ten years, I would buy beer, cigarettes, coffee, smoothies, burekas, and burritos with crumpled-up dollars people tossed into my case. Transmuting music into beer was magical; more exhilarating was the fact that I could now offer something to the world that made people smile.

Once I'd practiced alone in a room. Now, playing in public became its own religious ritual of connection. I'd find the just-right spot on a sunny street. Stand for a moment. Bend over to open my violin case, unstrap the Velcro that held its neck in place, turn the knob that held my bow, and pull them both from the case. Then I'd start playing, and see what happened.

I could never know who would walk by, how they'd treat me. Sometimes a person stopped and listened until I finished the song, then tossed me a dollar and said, "Hey, you're pretty good." Sometimes they said, "Fuck you." Once, in Massachusetts, a woman said apologetically, "Your music is beautiful, but I am a psychologist with an office on the second floor above where you are playing, and it is distracting to my patients."

It was vulnerable, standing there on the street corner with my case open. I tried my best to make grumpy passersby smile, figured out how to nod and say *Thank you* without stopping the tune. Sometimes, if a little kid was particularly curious, I would show them how to make a sound on the violin, bending down, letting them hold my instrument with their grubby hands. I unlearned every bit of technique I'd painstakingly drilled into my wrists and fingers, and in its place, I learned how to make toddlers dance on the sidewalk.

Busking was a practice of magic for me: how to magnetize the air around me, how to turn time into something as corporeal as challah dough, and braid my consciousness into strangers'. Where there is music, people gather. Music transforms the air as stained glass filters light. An ordinary room becomes a cathedral, a simple room becomes a sanctuary, a street becomes a holy place.

~

That was also the year I found God in a movie theater.

Following my principle of doing things that terrified me, I'd signed up for a semester at sea, sailing a wooden schooner for six weeks with strangers. I wanted to see what happened if I traded New York City for the unknown. I wanted to face my fear of waves pulling me under, my childhood tsunami panic; to feel my body against the vastness. And indeed, those six weeks at sea were a lesson in scale. I played fiddle on deck as the sun set, and the grand cycles of day and night out at sea showed me how small my world was, how vast the planetary distances.

When I returned to New York City, I knew how to shoot the moon with a sextant for celestial navigation. I could read the stars. And if I closed my eyes, I saw dolphins trailing the boat at night, braiding their green bioluminescent streams through the water. Even on the concrete of New York, I could still feel the rocking waves beneath my feet.

So when the movie *Titanic* came out, and I walked down Broadway to see it alone, and the ship hit the iceberg—when her hull split in two like a banana—when one half began to sink rapidly, pulling the second half after it, my throat seized in fear. I could feel myself on that deck, the freezing water waiting below.

On the part of the deck still above water, a string quartet played "Nearer, My God, to Thee." I watched, wide-eyed, unable to move. Beside them, a preacher cried out: "Save us, God!" Shaking, shivering, screaming, holding his arms to the sky: "Dear God, save us!"

So often I'd played my violin on the teak deck, my shipmates gathered around me in silence. In that moment, though, it hit me: If I were the violinist on *Titanic,* and the ship was sinking, I would stop playing and run to the preacher. I'd fling my violin away, let it be swallowed by the sea, and wail and pray.

Broadway was a river of taxis with their red lights trailing behind them when I left the theater. A cold drizzle fell on the city as I walked north, trembling. I felt my helplessness as a human animal, my impossible frailty. Something deep in me cried out in recognition of my own extinction.

Prayer, in that moment, came into focus as something entirely different from whispering prescribed words. Instead, it was an animal cry, a guttural relaxation of the illusion of control. This impulse to call out had something to do with accepting the power of the sea, the vast sky we sailed beneath, night after night, all that was beyond us. And it had something to do with relinquishing my own sense of self, giving in to something beyond me, joining its power.

I stopped to huddle under the roof of a bodega and rolled a cigarette. Was this prayer, then? Was *this* the point of all those words in the siddur? Was this what it meant to talk to God?

I leaned against the bodega window, sheltering beneath the awning, and it struck me: If this was prayer, why wait for a disaster? Why not talk to God in the most casual moments . . . like when walking home from a movie, smoking a cigarette?

I held the match close to my face and breathed in the sharp tobacco. As I walked home, I began to experiment:

Hi, God. I went to see a movie. (Pause.) *Thank you for the ocean. Thank you for not making the boat sink.* (Pause.) *Thanks for my violin. Thanks for New York City.* (Pause. Drag.) *Um, God . . . I think I might want to start getting to know you.*

Hannah

(1 Samuel)

What is prayer?

Or, stated differently: What is the balance between the power of claiming the truth and importance of our individual experience, and the power of acknowledging our insignificance in the face of the unimaginably vast universe?

Hannah is one of the most important models for prayer in the Jewish tradition. She's one of many women in the Torah who wants a child but cannot conceive—both a fact of her story and a metaphor for all human helplessness in the face of fate, biology, and the sometimes punishing fact of living in a body.

Her husband is supportive and kind, but no matter how much he reassures her that she is enough, Hannah is miserable. All her energy is focused on her desire for a child, and, adding insult to injury, she is constantly taunted by her über-fertile sister-wife, Penina.

But then a shift happens. After years of suffering, and from the depths of her despair, Hannah decides to take action by speaking directly to God.

She enters the Temple alone and begins to pray. Not gently, but deeply, wildly, with such intensity that the High Priest, Eli, thinks she's intoxicated. He reprimands her and sends her away, a profoundly unfair shaming: she's made herself vulnerable, prayed from the heart, and the man who is supposed to represent Divine authority responds with "Go home, you're drunk."

What power could she possibly have in this situation? At this point in the story, modern reader that I am, I'd expect Hannah—a woman in a patriarchal world, who's just been shamed by the High Priest—to return to her home in even greater despair.

But that's not Hannah's style. Instead, she defends herself to Eli. She wasn't drunk, she explains to him; she was just praying very, very hard.

And Eli, the High Priest, listens. This is one of the surprisingly frequent biblical moments in which a powerful man admits that a woman is right and he's wrong. "God will answer your prayer," Eli tells Hannah, and soon Hannah becomes pregnant. (It's worth noting that she's dedicated this son to God and has to give him away when he comes of age—Hannah gets what she wants, but at a price.)

Hannah's story doesn't end there, though, because she becomes the model for one of the most important Jewish prayers.

Here is where mythic and recorded history meet: centuries after Hannah's story is passed down, in 70 CE, the Romans destroy the Temple. Without a central altar, the entire system of priestly sacrifice—ancient Jews' primary mode of worship—evaporates. The ancient rabbis scramble to invent a new way to connect with God, and they come up with what we now know as Jewish prayer, recited by individuals and groups three times a day in place of the altar offerings. In search of a model for this new spiritual technology, they settle on Hannah, using her actions as the basis for how we recite one of the most important prayers, the Amidah.

The rabbis spell it out in the Talmud: When we stand before God in prayer, we can't simply recite the words they've written—we each have to add our own. They leave a space in the middle of the standardized language of the Amidah, and instruct us to whisper our own personal prayers into that silence. Like Hannah's, our lips move, but no sound comes out. Like Hannah, we lose ourselves a little bit and unspool our deepest prayers. Like Hannah, we let go of politeness and go deep into our true desires, whatever they may be—even if only for a moment.

Her story vibrates in the way we hold our bodies, the way we shape words with our lips, the way we express the wishes of our hearts.

But prayer is not only supplication. As described in Hannah's story, and elsewhere in the tradition of commentary, it is also a form of demand. A confrontation with what is, in the name of what could be. An act of imagination, of vulnerability, of strength, of holding two truths at once: our insignificance in the cosmic sense, and the deep significance of what lives in our hearts.

Caryatids and Torah

Early autumn again, the Upper West Side of Manhattan. The seasons moved through their cycles as I moved through college, and now it was my last year. Copper-colored maple leaves floated down onto the hexagonal paving stones lining Riverside Park; cars on Broadway endlessly offered their oceanic background noise; every Monday and Wednesday I bought a steaming bagel-egg-and-cheese sandwich from the vendor outside the college gates and ate it as I hurried to Chaucer class, my hands wrapped around the warm aluminum foil.

The end of college was in sight, and I'd still never had a real relationship—Boner didn't count—but I'd had plenty of non-relationships. Hooking up was a complicated negotiation, but I couldn't imagine any other way of doing things.

By now I'd learned the rules: how to slip away from boys who wanted to be more than friends when I didn't, while trying to wear down the resistance coming from other boys *I* wanted, who didn't want me that way. I'd pined for girls who only liked boys, and girls who only liked girls who only liked girls, and girls who were happy to spend the night but then pretended in the morning that nothing had happened. I'd politely declined both boys and girls who weren't my type. I'd been the needy one and the slippery one, the open one and the closed one, the one whose mind changed halfway through a kiss and the one watching as someone else walked away.

And then there was Zoe.

Shy and whip-smart, with pale skin and hazel eyes, she always sat in the front of Chaucer class. Her long thick auburn hair was a calm waterfall, ending just below her waist. Every day she wore the same thing: green army jacket, black leather pants, no makeup. Her lip trembled a little bit all the time. I couldn't stop thinking about her.

One day in October, our professor (sweetly butch, with a streak of purple in her short gray hair) asked for volunteers to make a banner for the poetry reading series. We both raised our hands, then shared a quick embarrassed glance. Was it possible she had been watching me too? I felt dizzy.

After class, our professor handed us the supplies: a cheap white bedsheet, permanent markers, and a pair of industrial scissors to cut U-shaped holes in the sheet, so the wind wouldn't turn it into a sail when they hung it. We sat cross-legged on the courtyard's sun-warmed bricks, the blank sheet spread out in front of us. After a long silence, Zoe said, "Let's draw a caryatid." I stared at her blankly. "You know," she said, "one of those pillars that's in the shape of a woman, like in a Greek building. Like a goddess holding up the roof."

We drew the caryatid together, crouching on the brick walkway. Her robes echoed the lines of the sheet. POETRY SERIES, we wrote underneath her in large black letters. As she moved the marker across the fabric, Zoe's hair brushed my wrist. We didn't quite finish the lettering, and we agreed to meet the next week after class.

∾

A few days later, I came back from orchestra rehearsal to find my roommate, Lily, and her best friend, Sarah, kneeling on the floor, wearing their Pavement and Guided by Voices T-shirts, seven-inch records covering the linoleum. I smiled; Lily (Korean American, sociology major) and Sarah (Jewish American, English major) were united in their geeky, encyclopedic command of obscure indie bands, and every Monday they spent hours preparing for their radio show, which was Tuesday mornings from three to four a.m.

"Hey," I said as I dropped my backpack on my bed, and they both looked up at me and waved. Though I'd seen Sarah a hundred times, today something about her outfit struck me. She was wearing a long denim skirt, and I suddenly realized that I'd *only* ever seen her in a long skirt. Everyone else I knew wore pants most of the time—worn corduroys, boyfriend jeans, vintage trousers. But not Sarah. Could she be Orthodox, like the girls who stood outside the sliding glass doors, waiting for me to walk through on Shabbat?

I tried to sound casual. "Hey, Sarah? Weird question. Are you wearing that skirt because you're Orthodox, or do you just like long skirts?"

"Ha. Yeah, I'm Orthodox. Modern Orthodox."

I didn't know what this meant, but I pressed on. "Can I ask you something? Do you wait until someone else walks through the sliding glass doors downstairs on Shabbat?"

"Uh, yeah . . . why?" I saw Sarah tense slightly, and I tensed in response. Had I said something wrong?

"Well, I just . . . I'm Jewish, but I don't know that much about it, and I . . . guess I'm curious."

"Oh." Sarah relaxed. Then she turned back to the latest Moldy Peaches release, and shrugged. "You should go to Wednesday Night Learning next week. It's on the top floor of Philosophy Hall. Just show up. They'll tell you what to do."

I said I'd think about it.

~

After Chaucer class the next week, Zoe and I finished the banner, carefully coloring in the last of the bubble letters with our thick black markers, a little dizzy from the scent. Then Zoe invited me to see her dorm room. She boiled water in an electric kettle and we drank Earl Grey tea together, making conversation, awkwardly at first and then more comfortably.

We talked until the stars came out and the campus quieted and even the sound of traffic outside began to die down. Then I took her hand, looked into her gray eyes, and kissed her. In the morning, I woke up to her breath on my neck, the tiny blonde hairs on her upper lip tickling my skin.

After that, we spent most nights together. Zoe climbed me like a tower, holding on to the windowsill to support herself. She let herself go with an adorable look of pain on her face, her copper hair sweeping my belly. She quivered in my arms, furrowed her forehead. We were no longer teenagers, but we were still shy around each other. We never took off our underpants, as if there were an unspoken agreement between us.

~

The next Wednesday, I climbed up the three flights of marble stairs, following the signs to a dusty marble hallway that felt like it contained centuries of philosophy lectures. Pulling the large, heavy door open, I felt a blast of heat and light, like opening a sauna door in winter.

I was late. The room was loud. Wednesday Night Learning had already started.

Three long tables stretched all the way to the back of the room, along which people sat in pairs. Each pair leaned together over an open book, reading out loud, pausing to consider, then speaking loudly to each other—heads bobbing, gesturing wildly, raising voices to be heard above the din, all of which made a roiling bed of sound and motion.

Pairs of young men with black hats and *peyes* identifying them as highly religious. Pairs of young women in skirts and long-sleeved shirts, their eyes animated with the same fire as the men. Large maroon books with golden Hebrew letters on the covers. They seemed to shimmer with knowledge of another world. I could hardly believe we were in the same room as those books.

As my eyes adjusted, I saw there were a few people who looked like me, too—piercings, weird haircuts, torn stockings. People I might have expected to see in a bar, not here, in this alternate universe of holy books scattered like treasure across the long tables.

A question mark opened up inside me, a new blank space just below my rib cage. Did this mean there was a passageway between my world and whatever this was?

I stood shyly just inside the doors for a few minutes, shifting from foot to foot as chatter and exclamations swirled around me. I looked down at my purple T-shirt, my worn jeans, my clear plastic lace-up shoes, my black-and-white-checkered socks. I waited. Something had to happen.

Then a skinny, pimply guy with white fringes hanging from his waistband saw me standing alone and ran toward me with great excitement. He was supercharged, a human exclamation point with a yarmulke. "Hey!" he shouted over the din. "Welcome! Are you here for Wednesday Night Learning? Do you need a *chavruta*?"

"What?" I yelled back.

"A study partner! Let's go find one for you!" He darted off into the sea of people, and I was alone again.

I had forgotten how it felt to be a first-year, stumbling through the early weeks of college with question marks around every corner: What is a registrar, where is the English Department, which of the bagel-and-coffee stands on Broadway has the best breakfast? Three years later, I knew my way around, at least outside this room. What was I doing here? I could just turn around and walk out, back into the world where I knew what words meant. I began to edge toward the door.

But before I could leave, the skinny guy returned, even more excited. Walking behind him was a girl with thick copper hair and creamy skin. She wore a long black skirt, a dark green cashmere sweater, and tiny gold studs in her ears. Somehow she managed to exude both preternatural calm and nervousness, an odd combination.

"I found you a *chavruta*! This is Shira! Have fun!" Exclamation Point chirped, and disappeared for good.

I immediately began to confess my ignorance, straining to yell over the din. "Hey, I should tell you . . . I'm Jewish, but I don't really know anything. I mean, I had a bat mitzvah, but that's it. I don't even know what I'm doing here." Shira's face filled with joy and purpose.

And so my twin studies, which would carry me through my senior year of college, began. With Shira I apprenticed in the school of mind and soul; with Zoe, in the school of body and heart.

My First *Chavruta*

I followed Shira to the other side of the room, squeezing through the alley of backpacks and chairs, dodging gesticulating hands, until we reached the bookshelf. It was filled with burgundy books, silver and gold Hebrew letters running down their spines. Shira chose one that had English letters as well as Hebrew. She pulled it off the shelf and squinted, surveying the room for empty seats. "Over there, come on!" She grabbed my elbow as if we were old friends and led me back through the crowd to the last two empty seats.

"Okay!" She beamed triumphantly as we sat down. Who was this person? I'd never met anyone so chipper; already I was beginning to find her enthusiasm exhausting. Once again I wondered what I was doing here.

"This is called *chavruta* learning," Shira chirped. "*Chavruta* means 'partner,' it comes from the word *chaver,* which means 'friend.' You're my *chavruta* now and I'm yours. We're going to learn together. We're going to start with Pirkei Avot. You'll love it."

Pirkei Avot turned out to be a series of short, aphoristic sayings from two thousand years ago, and it turned out that Shira was right. I did love these pieces of advice, which veered from practical advice to mystical, from pious to psychedelic.

> *Know where you come from, and where you are going, and before whom you are destined to give an account. From where do you come? From a putrid drop. Where are you going? To a place of dust, of worm and of maggot. Before whom are you destined to give an account and reckoning? Before the King of the Kings of Kings, the Holy One, blessed be.*

I sensed a sheen of antiquity, felt long-dead mouths forming around these words, and it gave me chills: the sheer scope of them, the way they zoomed out beyond a single lifetime, beyond a thousand thousand lifetimes, to see the beginning and end of all life. The grossness of the putrid drop and the maggots, the majesty of being called to account for my life. It made no sense, but it made perfect sense.

> *Let the property of your fellow be as precious unto you as your own; make yourself ready to study Torah, for it will not be yours by inheritance alone; and let all your actions be for the name of heaven.*

Look beyond your own self-interest, they were saying. Look beyond the bounds of your fragile ego, your ideas of what is yours. Everyone is precious, equally so. And the Torah may have been mine by inheritance, but that wasn't enough; I needed to make myself ready to study it. *Yes,* I thought, *make yourself ready.* I was young enough not to worry about what I'd be allowed to carry into this world, what I might be asked to give up.

In the following weeks, Shira and I met at Wednesday Night Learning. In two-hour sessions, she brought me into the world of these books. These sayings we studied together were called *mishnas,* she told me; they'd been transmitted orally for centuries before finally being written down. So many years, centuries, so many bodies reciting these words. I felt that process in the texts themselves: like stones washed clean by centuries of river water, any extra worn off, they spoke directly to me as I read out loud with Shira, wearing my grape-colored T-shirt, my lip ring.

The work is not yours to complete, nor are you free to desist from it.

I didn't yet know this was one of the most famous quotes from Jewish text; I just felt its truth, resonating like a copper bell through me. I'd grasped toward this before, practicing scales in front of a music stand, or entertaining passersby on the street. I'd felt it watching my father pursue the science of memory, his dedication and humility in knowing he was one of a chain of researchers working to understand the human mind. I'd seen it in Mrs. O'Brien's ingathering of weird teenagers into the art room, year after year, teaching us how to grow from children into adults who understood beauty. There would always be more work to do, we were each part of a bigger project; but the work in front of us was ours to do.

Which is the right path for a person to choose for themselves? Whatever is harmonious for the one who does it, and harmonious for humankind.

Reading these words, I felt the relief of counsel, of wisdom, of stepping into a tradition. A great peace began to spread through me, and a fatigue, a weight I had not known I was carrying, began to dissipate; it lifted from me like a cloud.

One who learns from his friend a single chapter, or a single law, or a single verse, or a single word, or even a single letter, he must treat him with respect.

Shira, my *chavruta,* my new friend, had led me to a treasure chest marked with my name, which I had not known existed until this moment.

Rabbi Shimon said . . . do not view yourself as a bad person.

I'd thought the rabbis would focus on laws and rules and how to be a better person and how to love God more. Instead, here was Rabbi Shimon, whoever that was, telling me to love myself as I was.

What else did those books hold between their mahogany covers?

The Daughters of Tzelofchad

(Book of Numbers)

When I learned to read those texts, I found much of what I'd always assumed would be in the holy books: laws and rules, how to be better, how to love God more. And, yes, slavery and patriarchy and a jealous, judgmental Divine wove through the texts like insistent, itchy threads.

But also, I found such unexpected beauty in the stories.

Sometimes that beauty is emotional, like the tearful reconciliation between long-estranged brothers. Sometimes it's spiritual, like the night a man wrestles with an angel until dawn, and receives a blessing for his courage. And sometimes, it's simply the beauty of good politics—as in the story of the daughters of Tzelofchad, in which five sisters recognize injustice, and work together to change the laws.

The Israelites are in a moment of transition, still wandering in the desert but getting close to the Promised Land. God has declared that when the Israelites arrive in the Land of Israel, ownership will be apportioned tribally, with amounts based on the census of each tribe. (The question of who was already living there, and what it meant to declare ownership over the land once the Israelites arrived, is not considered within this text, but as a modern reader I hold it in my mind.)

In this liminal moment, a man named Tzelofchad dies. He leaves behind five daughters—Mahlah, Noah, Hoglah, Milcah, and Tirzah. But since only men are counted in the census, and Tzelofchad has no sons, his daughters will not inherit property when they arrive in the Promised Land. This affects not only the daughters, but their entire tribe, which will receive a smaller portion of land.

In response to this injustice, the five sisters become legal activists. They petition Moses for their right to inherit, Moses consults God, and God decides that their claim is valid. Not only will the five daughters themselves receive their father's land, but a precedent is set for female inheritance—at least in some cases.

This ethical triumph is limited. Daughters can inherit land only when there are no sons, and then they are required to marry within their tribe; once married, the land follows the male spouse. This is a patriarchal society, after all. Still, God recognizes the daughters' argument, and in response, inheritance law is changed.

This story belongs to the surprising genre of Torah stories in which women, at first denied power, figure out a way to advocate for themselves, and emerge victorious. Sometimes these women work outside the system, sometimes within it; the daughters of Tzelofchad are in the latter group. Their strategy is not as cinematic as some of the others, who run away from their home of origin (Rachel), or kill an enemy with a tent peg through the temple (Yael), or put on a veil and seduce a withholding man who owes them a baby (Tamar). Instead, the five sisters simply approach Moses with a legal argument—and it works.

Perhaps the sisters learned this strategy of working within the system from their father; Tzelofchad lived in the tumultuous generation of Korach, a populist who attempted a violent revolution against Moses. Korach was considered so dangerous to the unity of a ragtag band of ex-slaves that God destroyed him and his followers. (Though you could certainly argue, as many have, that God should have been more compassionate toward Korach and his questions.)

In their appeal, Tzelofchad's daughters specify that Tzelofchad was a contemporary of Korach, but *not* one of his followers. Perhaps this is why when his daughters challenge Moses and the established power structure just one generation later, their methods are more nuanced, and so is the response.

Besides the political implications, there is another, more existential thread in this story: the question about what happens when we are gone. Will anyone remember us? Will our tribe continue? Will civilization survive?

This is, after all, what inheritance is about. On a literal level, the daughters are agitating for land rights, but on a more metaphysical level, they are arguing for the right to be heard—for their story to exist. Will they be swallowed in silence, or will their stories echo through time?

Mahlah, Noah, Hoglah, Milcah, and Tirzah. Interesting that these five sisters' names are passed down to us through millennia, while Bat Yiftach, whose tale is longer and carries life-and-death stakes, is called simply "Yiftach's daughter." Might this be because the sisters demanded to be heard? Is this how we name ourselves—by questioning what we are told to accept, discerning our inner sense of truth, and speaking it out loud?

Whether the five sisters existed in history or simply in myth, their story represents the fact that *someone*—probably many people—were courageous and tenacious enough to change the way that property, information, power, and tradition were passed down. And that our ancestors thought it was important to pass their story on to us, as if to say, The tradition was never static. You, too, will need to co-create it.

The work was not theirs to complete, nor were they free to desist from it. And now it is our turn: to pass on their stories and to live our own; to wrestle with the tradition and reinterpret it toward more justice, more love; to discern the truth that lives inside us, and speak it out loud.

A Crash Course in Holiday Rules

Okay: no driving, no phones, no turning lights on or off. Basically, no electricity of any kind." Shira paused for a minute, thinking. "And no hot water, because it makes the water heater start up again."

The northern suburbs sped by in a red-and-gold blur. We were on the train up to Connecticut to spend Rosh Hashanah at her parents' house, and Shira was giving me a crash course in the holiday rules.

"Let's see: no writing, no cooking, obviously no fire, no smoking"—sidelong glance.

Rosh Hashanah is a two-day holiday; this year, Shira explained, Shabbat happened to be the next day, so we would be observing these rules for seventy-two hours. It was going to be my first time in an Orthodox house.

"Oh, and on Shabbat, don't carry anything outside the house, but you can during Rosh Hashanah."

Shira's family lived in a commuter suburb; most of the fathers—and a few mothers—took the train to New York City each day to work and returned home at night. During the eighty-minute ride, Shira told me about her family. "They're Modern Orthodox," she explained, sighing a bit, as the trees blurred by. I nodded. Modern Orthodox: like Sarah, like the girls who waited outside the sliding glass doors on Friday night. One foot in the world of the Torah, the other in the world I lived in.

"My mom went to Stern, the women's Orthodox college in New York. She kept kosher and kept Shabbos and everything, but on weekdays, she also, like, wore jeans and didn't cover her hair. And my dad wore a baseball cap instead of a kippah."

I understood. Her parents observed the Torah laws, but they wanted to blend in too.

"But," Shira said, her eyes flashing, "I don't really understand why they think it's okay to follow *most* of the laws but not *all* of them."

I'd grown up thinking of Orthodox Judaism as one monolithic bloc of the faithful and slightly crazed, which was how my parents thought of it, and probably their parents too, none of us having had more than incidental contact with Orthodox Jews. But Shira showed me that Orthodox Judaism, like everything else human, contains vast gradations. Just as our Reform synagogue growing up had families who baked challah every Friday and gathered for long Passover seders, and families like us who schlepped across town only on the very holiest days when we felt ourselves required to show up to perform the minimum obeisance to a God we didn't really believe in, Orthodoxy was a continuum.

After graduating from her all-girl Modern Orthodox high school, Shira had enrolled in her mother's alma mater, but chose to spend the traditional "seminary year" in Israel first, studying Torah before college. There, amidst the echo of millennia, the dusty hills and sacred sites, holiness palpable in the air, Shira decided she no longer wanted the "modern" part of Modern Orthodox.

She believed every word of the Torah, and she wanted to live every word. She wanted it all: the husband, the many children, the sleeves down to her wrists, the skirts down to her ankles. She returned from seminary, gave away her old immodest V-neck T-shirts, and asked her family to refrain from discussing worldly matters at the holy Shabbat table.

Her parents were horrified. "But you're so smart," her mother had said. "You have so much potential." As far as Shira's parents were concerned, she'd become an extremist, and without an intervention they feared she'd sign her life away to some twenty-one-year-old yeshiva student; in a year, she'd be married, pregnant, and working full-time to support the family while her husband studied.

So her parents made a decision. Shira would transfer from the Orthodox women's college to Barnard, my college, two miles up Broadway. It was a good compromise, because it was a secular university with many Modern Orthodox students. So Shira would sit in class each day with pious, scholarly girls like her—who went on chaste dates with boys in yarmulkes, assessing each other openly as marriage partners, discussing the numbers of children they planned to have, God willing—and with rebellious feminists with shaved heads and septum rings, who hung out downtown at the dyke bars.

Which pretty much summed up Shira and me. And now Shira was bringing me home for three straight days of Modern Orthodox holiday rules.

∾

Shira's parents welcomed me warmly. Their house was impeccably clean, plush, and suburban, the kitchen gleaming. When she took me upstairs to drop off my bags, I saw that her bedroom was decorated like a young girl's: pink rug, pink sheets, two twin beds on opposite walls.

During dinner, after we lit the candles and said the blessings and ate the holiday meal with apples and honey and round challah, I excused myself to pee. It was the heavenly bathroom of a family of strangers: pink soap in the shape of a shell, soft white towels on the rack.

I lifted my hand to pull toilet paper from the roll but stopped myself abruptly: Shira had explained to me that her mother would have pre-ripped toilet paper and left it on the top of the toilet tank. "Use that," she said, "because we don't cut or tear on the holiday." I twisted my torso around and there it was: a neat stack of toilet paper, four squares per piece. I lifted one and brought it fluttering down between my legs, feeling holy as I wiped.

Then I froze. Were you allowed to flush on a holiday? I couldn't remember Shira mentioning it, but it seemed to fit in the list of forbidden actions. And the bathroom was close enough to the dining room that everyone would hear my desecration.

I quietly closed the toilet lid, washed my hands with cold water, and returned to the table. Later, when we were alone, I asked Shira and she laughed with delight. "Oh yes, of *course* you can flush the toilet!" she said, beaming. I felt equal parts pride for displaying my burgeoning piety, and embarrassment—how little I knew of this world.

We walked to synagogue, since driving was forbidden on the holiday, and I experienced walking as a sacred act for the first time. I would have expected an Orthodox neighborhood to be filled with strange sounds and smells, but this looked like the place I grew up—neat suburban streets, trees, houses. My awareness, though, was different. Once again I had that sense of tingling consciousness I'd felt outside my dorm, watching the girls wait for the sliding glass doors to open. But this time I was inside the holiness, walking instead of driving, inhabiting the invisible magic of a holy day, the subtle intention of pre-ripped toilet paper, of knowing the cars would stay parked for days. As if someone had pulled the plug on the mechanical world, the drudgery of machinery and products, and only the human was allowed here.

On the way, Shira explained that her family and their other guests would attend services upstairs in the main sanctuary, while I'd be downstairs in a different service called the learners' minyan. "You'd be bored up here," she told me, and her mother nodded in agreement beside her. "Yes, we'll walk you down. It'll be much better for you."

The learners' minyan was held in a small basement classroom, the walls decorated with bright cutouts of Hebrew letters. A divider on wheels, about as high as my head, split the room down the middle, with women on one side and men on the other. Shira gestured for me to join the women's side, where seven of us stood awkwardly with our bilingual prayer books. I was the youngest. The leader stood at the front of the room, at the head of the divider, so both sides could see him equally. He was about sixty years old—kind, patient, welcoming—and he took care to direct his words toward the women as well as the men. "We turn to page thirty-seven and recite the Shema," he said. "The declaration of the Oneness of Hashem."

Shema Yisrael, Adonai eloheinu, Adonai echad. Hear O Israel, the Lord is our God, the Lord is One. One of the few prayers I learned growing up. The same melody I sang as a child.

I felt dizzy, as if a thread were being pulled through me, the familiar stitched to the deeply foreign, the fabric of my childhood tied suddenly to this world. As if I were an anthropologist who had traveled far to study a tribe and, observing their ceremony, found they were reciting the Pledge of Allegiance I grew up saying each morning in elementary school.

I followed along for most of the service, equal parts moved and bored. I was certain the real action was upstairs in the grand sanctuary, where they recited the full liturgy, mumbling in Hebrew, knowing every word. Meanwhile, down in the basement we stumbled through a shortened version; I was embarrassed by my inexperience, my ignorance of our tradition, the childishness of my mispronounced prayers.

Afterward, we walked back home together through the quiet streets of their Orthodox neighborhood, Shira's family calling out holiday greetings to the families and couples we passed, all on their way home from services. Then, at dinner, after the blessings had been chanted, round challahs sliced and dipped in honey, apple slices drizzled with honey brought to our lips, prayers offered for a sweet new year, Shira's whole family turned to me.

"How was it at the learners' minyan?" they asked as they passed silver platters of green beans and carrots and fish. I expected their curiosity to be polite and brief, but the questions continued, genuine and loving. "What did you think? Did you like it? What did you learn?"

I answered honestly—"so interesting, I really liked it, I learned we blow the shofar one hundred times"—though I couldn't understand why they would care. Why did it matter what I thought about the watered-down versions of the prayers I'd been stumbling through in the basement, when they'd been fluently reciting the real versions in the magnificent sanctuary upstairs?

Now, all these years later, I think I understand. Seen through another's eyes, our own culture leaps to life. Theirs was the curiosity of a family hosting an international exchange student, asking at the dinner table—*Do you like it here? What does our life look like to you? Can you help us understand ourselves?*

Or perhaps it was something else. We were all Ashkenazi Jews, and for all I knew, we were distant cousins; how easily we could have been living each other's lives, if our respective grandparents had settled on a different level of piety and assimilation.

But instead—thanks to fate, social pressure, or an accident of history—we lived in different worlds. It was like looking in a mirror at an alternate version of our own lives.

Or maybe they were just making conversation to welcome the stranger who had come to join their table for the holiday, as so often happens in the stories of the shtetl. In the glowing light, we talked and laughed, dipping apple slices in honey, celebrating the New Year in early fall, as our ancestors had for so many centuries.

∾

For those three days, I felt like I'd walked through a portal into another world, entered a video game where treasures gleamed beneath the desert sand and oracles waited around every corner to instruct me. Something in me knew I would return to this world, to follow paths I'd only glimpsed, uncover wisdom I'd only tasted briefly.

But also: I missed Zoe and her long auburn hair. I missed my own bed. I missed my weird artist friends, our shared references, the wordless understanding of playing music together. After three days in this magical, sacred universe, I was itching to return to my regular life.

The Earth Wobbles on Its Axis

Talmud is like baseball," Shira said, looking dreamily out the window as the September trees blurred by on the train ride back to the city. After three days eating and praying together, three nights sleeping in twin beds on opposite sides of her plush pink room, we still had almost nothing in common, two strangers whose lives had improbably crossed for a moment. But she loved to teach me, and I loved to learn.

Think about baseball, Shira explained: If you don't know the rules, it seems sort of silly and sad, a bunch of grown men running around after a little ball. But learn the game, and you understand its elegance, see it for what it really is—a practice, another human way of reaching toward the infinite. "It's magic." She turned to me, a hand on my shoulder. "You'd love it. The Talmud is like nothing else, this huge book of stories, laws, arguments, and even gossip, all written down around fifteen hundred years ago."

Those oversized, rectangular volumes with glowing gold letters on mahogany covers, which drew me like a magnet when I first walked into Wednesday Night Learning—that, Shira said, was Talmud. Inside those books, ancient Hebrew mixed with Aramaic, compressed into a sort of code. Columns of text wrapped around each other, commenting, elucidating and embracing each other, written in varied sizes and scripts depending on which scholar contributed them.

For centuries, Talmud had been the province of men. In recent years, though, Modern Orthodox girls had been permitted to study it. Shira got a taste, and fell in love. But, as her parents reminded her regularly, the ultra-Orthodox world she yearned to enter forbade women from studying Talmud. And she admitted it to me: because she was a woman, Shira's very devotion to studying sacred texts was what held her back from becoming truly fundamentalist (or in her own words, "totally frumming out").

∾

The tall trees of Westchester County segued into the tall concrete buildings of New York City as we barreled south in the silver train. I couldn't wait to see Zoe. I wanted to tell her about the basement prayers and the round challahs dipped in honey and Shira's all-pink bedroom. I wanted her to help me understand who I was becoming.

As a child, I had a recurring nightmare that I was looking for small turquoise beads. On a school bus, in tangled grass, in a jewelry box. I never knew why I had to find the beads—only that I had to find them or something terrible would happen.

Now I had a name for the beads, a place to put them: tradition. A language to learn, a code to unlock, a whole map of rituals that could hold me and calm me from morning to night.

But still, so many questions. What constellation do these stars form: a lover's body under a red velvet bedspread; playing fiddle on a street corner; looking for God? Who planted this desire in me, this yearning to understand the world around me and inside me? And where would it lead?

~

All that year, I had two teachers.

On Wednesday nights, Shira instructed me in the ancient texts of my tradition. A new topography opened up, unseen but real, like the ocean floor, and Shira helped me map it. In this world, people spoke the questions I had always feared were too big, unseemly in their ambition: How should we live? What does it mean to be good? Where do I end, and where does everything else begin? The letters began to awaken on the page, to stretch and jostle their margins. They rose up to meet me, and all their questions had more than one answer.

The other nights of the week, Zoe taught me to open the secret doors of my body. Twenty years old—delirious, impatient, grateful—we charted the terra incognita of our own bodies. We mapped sunlit glades, cool caves, mountaintops, gentle breezes, sea monsters who opened their mouths to reveal more pleasure glistening inside their throats.

We were each other's caryatids. We joked about how Jewish I was becoming, how soon I'd be wearing a wig. "I'm your shiksa," she said, laughing. I made her a tape and titled it "Shiksa Mix," writing the words carefully on the white-lined sticker; she smiled and threw her arms around me.

Zoe knew about Shira, and listened with love as I described my growing obsession with Judaism. She'd grown up in New Jersey and had been to more bar and bat mitzvahs than I had. The whole thing seemed more exotic to me than it did to her.

Shira, on the other hand, did not know about Zoe. I wasn't hiding our relationship, exactly, but I didn't want to shock my sweet *chavruta,* whose childhood bedroom was still intact, who had never kissed a boy and walked through the world with a sort of wide-eyed innocence.

Plus, even though Zoe and I were dating publicly, when it came to the wider world—Shira, my parents—keeping quiet about relationships with girls was still an easy reflex for me to slip into. Even the fairly progressive rabbinical school a few blocks up Broadway didn't accept openly queer students into its Conservative Jewish seminary, and another decade would pass before that policy changed. So how would Shira—sheltered, Modern-Orthodox-leaning-toward-ultra-Orthodox Shira—react to her *chavruta* coming out to her?

∾

But I wasn't the only one learning in our *chavruta,* and I couldn't keep Zoe a secret forever. While Shira was teaching me about her world of Jewish texts, I was also teaching her about the world outside Orthodoxy. After we finished studying a *mishna,* we'd sit and talk for a while in an unspoken trade, and often her questions had to do with dating:

S: So . . . since you don't have any modesty rules, do people just have sex on the first date?
A: I mean—sometimes, but not always, and it doesn't feel as crazy as it sounds.
S: Hm. Okay. So . . . can you really date two people at once?
A: Yeah. You can even fool around with two people at once!
S (blushing): Whoa. That is . . . Okay . . . I'm just . . . Okay wow.

One cold November night, as we walked back across campus after Wednesday Night Learning, Shira asked me if I was dating anyone. I breathed in deeply. "Well . . . yes, actually," I said, pretending not to be nervous, "a girl named Zoe."

A beat of silence, and I wondered: Would she stop studying with me? She was my door into this world. Without Shira, who would teach me Torah? Who could I ask?

Shira smiled and in her high, innocent voice, she said, "Why didn't you tell me you were dating someone? That's so exciting!"

Looking back, I wish I'd had the courage to continue this conversation with Shira. Did her mind flash to the ancient biblical prohibitions from Leviticus, which technically pass judgment only on sex between men, not women? (One of a number of areas where the traditional patriarchal focus allows women's experience to go relatively unremarked upon, keeping female queerness the tiniest bit safer, in theory if not in practice.) Did she consider that she, too, was questioning the assumptions she'd grown up with, the model her parents had created for her, as her own passion for God exceeded the boundaries her family had set? Was she afraid of losing me, as I was of losing her? Or was she simply inclined toward kindness and not judgment, and did as Rabbi Hillel suggested when asked to summarize Judaism in one sentence: "Don't do to your neighbor what you wouldn't want them to do to you. The rest is commentary."

In the moment, my heart thumping with adrenaline, I only felt relief as we both moved on to other topics. My *chavruta* with Shira stayed separate from my everyday life and loves; we didn't hang out socially, only met to study or observe holidays together. But her simple, gentle acceptance felt like a small trapdoor opening deeper into this world of Torah.

Shira and Zoe, Zoe and Shira. Their lessons intertwined in me, in the glistening organs of my body, the flying buttresses of my mind: lessons of pleasure and wisdom, the warp and weft of my twenty-first year.

~

Growing up, we learned that Polaris was the North Star. But in astronomy class, I'd learned that the earth wobbles on its axis, which means the North Star changes. The official term, our professor told us, is that the North Celestial Pole is *restless*—like a human, seeking meaning. Two thousand years from now, humans will look up at the night sky and point to a different North Star.

I thought back to my dream of searching for turquoise beads. In the dark, flying on instinct, we find one bead, then the next. *Try to love the questions themselves,* wrote Rilke.

Only in retrospect, years later, do the stars form a shape you can read in the sky, like an answer. And even the answer changes back into a question, if you give it a couple millennia.

When We're Born, We Forget Everything

I knew little of politics, or of the Bible, and Jerusalem had never interested me: just another distant, dusty, bloody metropolis half the globe away. So when I began to dream of the holy city during my senior year of college, it was not the modern Jerusalem—golden dome, gleaming white stone, buses and cars, crowded colorful markets. Instead, I dreamed of an inner Jerusalem: no city, just desert.

In these dreams, the desert was red, the red clay of Colorado, or maybe Mars. No buildings, no people; rust-colored earth as far as I could see. I approached the holy city in a helicopter. Was there a pilot? I didn't notice; the desert drew me down magnetically from the air, the propellers making circle patterns in the dust below.

The dream helicopter touched down, the door lifted, hot air rushed in. I stepped out onto ground and knelt on the hard earth, wind in my hair. I leaned over and kissed the blood-red ground. I could still feel tendrils of the dream after I woke up, and I knew that soon I would be in a different land.

∾

Shira was delighted by my dream. "You have to go," she chirped, "and I know exactly the place! This seminary in Jerusalem, well, in the hills outside the city. It's amazing!" Her voice dropped to a whisper. "You'll love it. It's all girls, and they understand that people are coming from different backgrounds."

The website promised a place of warm, welcoming knowledge, where young women were lovingly brought into the tradition while being intellectually challenged and spiritually supported. Every photo was full of young women in long skirts and long sleeves, sitting together at desks, bending over those magnetic holy books. I envied them, their fingers touching the letters.

I experienced my newfound faith as a desire for knowledge—a form of lust, almost. I wanted to touch the essence of life, to talk directly about what it meant to exist on this earth, and these books were full of those questions, maybe even a few answers. I wanted them in the same way I wanted people's bodies close to mine, my lips on theirs, their hands slipping inside the waist of my jeans.

It was my last spring at Barnard, and I'd talked my way into a graduate literature seminar, where I sat beside a thin, nervous, bespectacled grad student named Jacob. His comments tended toward the dark and bitingly ironic, but I could tell he was kind. One day in class, he mentioned that he'd lived in Jerusalem for a few years, and I cornered him after class: "Hey, do you know about this place for women to study Torah, in the hills, outside Jerusalem?"

Jacob snorted right in my face. "Ha! Yeah. American girls go there to turn Orthodox." Then he stopped and looked at me with horror. "Wait . . . you're not thinking about going there, are you?"

"Well, yeah." I shrugged. "This girl Shira said it would be great for me . . ."

"Oh God, no," Jacob said, shaking his head rapidly. "Steer clear.

Believe me, you'd hate that place. If you must go on your quest, there's a co-ed yeshiva on the other side of town. They just teach Torah there, instead of trying to convert everyone to Orthodoxy. At least they live in the modern world. That's the only place you'd survive. Don't listen to that girl."

Jacob was right—I knew it immediately. I was still a feminist, still my rational father's daughter, and my drive toward the sacred was accompanied by a powerful skepticism. I needed to study at a school that welcomed all of me: the part that loved the rules, and the part that pushed back against them. I looked up the yeshiva online; I'd missed their application deadline by a week. I wrote an email asking if I could possibly come study, and if so, could I also apply for all available scholarships and loans?

The acceptance letter came two weeks later, with one condition: If I was willing to spend the month of August in an intensive Hebrew program, I could begin yeshiva in September.

I didn't have the courage to tell Zoe directly that I had to leave her and seek something that I could only find alone. Instead, I withdrew slowly, without explanation, breaking up with her simply by retreating. All that I was studying about how to be a good person, yet I slunk away from a person I loved.

~

"Do you really believe all that mumbo jumbo?" my father said, when I told him I wanted to go to Jerusalem. Home for spring break, I fought with him in a way I hadn't since early high school, standing in the familiar yellow kitchen, surrounded by the rustic print of apples and leaves on the wallpaper. He was a doctor, a scientist, and I was entering the realm of mystery. "So if you can't drive on Shabbat, all the Jews have to live in the same neighborhood?" he said with disgust. "It's a tribal mentality, setting yourself apart. The ghetto. Closing yourself off to the rest the world."

Shira once taught me that a rope was tied around the body of the High Priest when he entered the Holy of Holies once a year, on Yom Kippur. The power in that curtained space was so blindingly bright that the High Priest would die on the spot if he were impure, and he wore the rope so the priests could drag his lifeless body out without entering the sanctum. It wasn't science, it was poetry: a place so holy that a life without integrity could kill you on the spot.

My father and I fought about going backward, about culture and superstition, about the violence of religious faith, about closed-mindedness and privilege, about what it means to be free.

The Talmud, Shira taught me, *says that every gestating baby has a candle hanging above it in the womb, and by this light an angel teaches the baby the entire Torah. But when we're born, we forget everything.*

"Where is all this leading?" my mother asked, concern in her eyes. "Are you going to refuse to eat in my kitchen because it's not kosher?" She was afraid I would go off the deep end, and I couldn't promise I wouldn't. "I mean . . . are you going to stop being able to hug your uncle, your cousins?"

I said: "I don't know. I'm sorry. I just have to go."

Miriam

(Book of Numbers)

Miriam has been beloved by the people since childhood. She is a prophetess, a priestess, a leader. Long ago, as a girl, she watched over baby Moses in his basket of reeds, risking her own life to keep her little brother safe. After crossing that terrible sea, she led the women in a song of praise. And in the desert, after the Exodus, she keeps them alive with her water magic, finding a well in each encampment. (So, at least, say the rabbis.)

But then her story swerves. The problem begins when Miriam and Aaron criticize their brother, Moses. *Has God spoken only through Moses? Has God not spoken to us as well?* And God's answer is swift and harsh. *How dare you question my chosen prophet, Moses? With him I speak mouth to mouth, only he beholds my Face.*

With these words, God erases Miriam's power, her history of service, transforming her from insider to outsider. Aaron is untouched, but Miriam's skin turns white as snow. In fairy tales, white skin signifies a pale, creamy beauty. Here, in this story from the Mediterranean, white means the opposite: disfigurement. Miriam's skin grows scaly, it appears to rot. And Moses, whom she has criticized, cries out in shock to see his older sister humiliated in this way. *O God, please heal her!* he calls out. *El na, refa na la!*

I will heal her, God says, *but not right away. For if her father spit in her face, wouldn't she have to bear her shame for seven days?* And God sends her out of the camp for a week.

Miriam is not the only one to be called into the wilderness by God. Moses, too, is commanded to leave the Israelites and enter the wilderness of Mount Sinai alone. But Moses's solitude is directed toward a sacred meeting, a moment of transformational intimacy with God. Miriam's is the opposite: she is sent out alone, abandoned, exiled.

God is not the only actor in this story, though. The Children of Israel have a collective voice, too. And they respond quite differently toward the absence of Moses and that of Miriam.

While Moses is up on the mountain receiving the Torah, the people lose patience. They seem to forget all about Moses, and, for that matter, God. They melt down their jewelry, sculpt a statue of a calf, and begin to worship it.

Miriam, though, is remembered in her absence. In fact, the people refuse to travel until she is gathered back into the community. They wait for her.

In the desert, the cycles are stark. The sun rises, the sun sets. The days are hot, the nights freezing. It is not hospitable for humans, but for spiders and scorpions it is home. The terrible predator dies one day and offers its body to the birds of prey. A drop of water glistens, balancing on the spike of a cactus. Inside the body of the cactus, water, enough to survive on its own.

And God? God is fluid across these stories. Sometimes a loving parent, a liberator, a leader, other times, a father who spits in your face. We humans, like Miriam, are fluid as well. Sometimes we hear the voice of God, sometimes not. Sometimes we are held, sometimes alone. Sometimes we wait for each other; sometimes we need to leave.

One Last Summer in Captivity

New York, 1998: my last heathen summer.

It was almost time for me to join my forefathers and foremothers, the journey of Abraham and of Ruth—to leave the home of one's youth and find God. But the immersive Hebrew program didn't start for two more months. So I, child and grandchild and great-grandchild of errant Jews, had one more heathen summer. I loved every minute of it.

I shared a tiny mice-infested studio apartment in the East Village with a dancer friend from college. We slept on twin mattresses on opposite sides of the room. We each kept a flashlight by our head to shine at the mice when they ventured out of the cupboards in the middle of the night, trying to keep them from our beds.

I broke a hundred religious laws every day, laws I did not yet know existed. I failed to pray three times a day, failed to tithe, to recite blessings each time I ate, to keep kosher, to give thanks after going to the bathroom. I coveted, I gossiped, ate potato chips and tuna sandwiches on fast days, transgressed the laws of sexual purity again and again. In other words, I lived the way I had been raised to live.

The ancient rabbis had a name for a person raised like me: *tinok shenishba,* a "captured infant." It is a term of compassion, springing from an ancient legal question: what to do in the case of a person who repeatedly violates the Sabbath, never having been taught otherwise.

Two thousand years ago, the ancient rabbis forgave me: *One who does not know that there is a commandment to observe Shabbat in the Torah, because they were captured as an infant, and as a result performs many prohibited labors on multiple Shabbats, is liable to bring only one sin-offering.*

In the twelfth century, Maimonides, Jewish scholar and doctor to the Sultan of Egypt, wrote: *The children of errant Jews and their grandchildren whose parents led them away and they were born among non-observers and raised according to their conception, they are considered as children captured and raised by them.*

I had grown up in the happy home of my parents, and yet I fit this description perfectly: raised in another culture, ignorant of the traditions. The freedom I was raised with, the rabbis were saying, was also a form of captivity. And the rules into which I longed to walk were a form of freedom.

Later I would find out that the opposite is true as well. Sometimes a child grows up in a tradition, carefully instructed in every last law, but she grows up to find that her true joy lies elsewhere; she must walk out of that castle and live her own bright life.

~

That summer, I worked at the Poetic Archives, which was housed in a historic mansion across the street from the city's only private park, in a fancy neighborhood I had no business being in. When I wasn't at work, I was writing in my journal at Alt.coffee, the grubby café a few blocks away, across the street from (the very public) Tompkins Square Park. Or sipping the bitter foam off my Guinness at the Irish dive bar across the street from our apartment. Or riding the powder-blue Schwinn I was bike-sitting for a friend. Or going to drag shows. But weekday mornings were always the same: I would take a cold shower to wash off the last night's sweat, put on a summer dress and sandals, unlock the Schwinn from the wrought iron in front of my walk-up, and ride a mile north to work.

The mansion that housed the nonprofit, a Victorian Gothic double town house of dark wood and pink marble, had been built for a wealthy governor of New York City in the late 1800s. Its dark wood held a sense of faded glory, the glamour of New York past, and I felt proud to walk through those mahogany doors, even if I was there for a minimum-wage office job. The lobby's polished wood gleamed and the first floor housed a fancy private club, but farther upstairs, out of sight of the members, the building was shabby and falling apart. From the stairway, I could look up and see the mansion's crown jewel: a Tiffany glass skylight, a glorious jumble of green, blue, and white glass shot through with sun. As if a stained glass window had migrated to the ceiling. As if the whole building were some sort of topsy-turvy cathedral to art.

The Poetic Archives office took up the whole third floor, the former maids' quarters, and had the feeling of a respectable literary punk house. A pocket door that never closed separated two giant rooms with wooden floorboards worn down to softness, no trace of polish left. Papers and books were piled everywhere; desktop computers, old issues of the organization's magazine, stacks of leftover programs from long-ago readings perched precariously on high shelves. Everything seemed to be sliding downward, propped up against other diagonals. I was still young enough that the disarray and decay felt romantic to me, not depressing.

The previous two summers, I'd worked answering phones in the overly air-conditioned Industrial Tower 3 in exurban Baltimore. There, when I'd sneak in a paperback of poems to read between phone calls, it felt like contraband—a glowing nugget of meaning smuggled into a refrigerator of capitalism. But at the Poetic Archives, poetry was the axis around which the office rotated, the lifeblood flowing through each day. My coworkers, all artists, were sensitive and dramatic, and I felt normal around them. *Works of art,* wrote the poet Rilke, *arise from an infinite aloneness;* my infinite aloneness felt manageable beside theirs. I began to wonder whether it really made sense for me to go all the way to Jerusalem, but it was too late now. *Just one year,* I told myself, *then back to regular life.*

That summer, I was reading T. S. Eliot. I loved his poems except for the religious parts; despite my own spiritual searching, I still had trouble contending with the word "God" in poetry. I could imagine a personal conversation with God walking up Broadway on a rainy night, but in classic poetry, "God" reverted to my childhood understanding: remote, hard, flat, judgmental, like a slab of marble. I sensed no possibility of conversation with that word, no love coming from it. I was hungry for wisdom, ritual, and the palpable sacred; the God of English literature felt to me like a judge, a distant father I had no interest in getting to know.

Yet some of my favorite poets used this word frequently, and for some reason, on this sweaty, midsummer Sunday, omnipresent car alarms bleeping outside my apartment window, I had an idea. What if I took everything I *did* believe in, or, more precisely, experienced—the beating sacredness of time, the vibration of electricity inside me, all that was beyond my control, the swooping multifarious power of forests, the relief of surrender, the *Titanic* sinking, Rabbi Shimon reaching out from two thousand years ago, telling me not to judge myself as a bad person—what if

I took all that, and, as my high school algebra teacher used to say, "plugged it in" to the variable of the word "God"?

I'd never liked math, but in that moment, algebra became a mechanism to unlock a profound secret. I performed the equation on poem after poem, swapping variables, and suddenly the poems popped off the page, shedding their fog to emerge, four-dimensional, five-dimensional. I breathed in deep, filled with love and oxygen up to my edges, my body an airy vessel of pleasure.

God. *God!* That suddenly kite-like, rainbowed word unfurled majestically, like a parachute, like streamers, filling the room, filling East Fifth Street and the city, the East River, the sky, the East Coast, the continent, globe, sun in the firmament, stars beyond which I could not see in the daytime brightness, but which I knew were there, as vast as my organs were small, but temporary like me, each of us in a brief moment of existence, made of hydrogen and matter. Mysterious system, sacred algebra.

From that moment on, I knew what people meant when they said, "I believe."

They Bury Their Dead on the Roof

In late July, my roommate and I packed up the apartment. It was an easy task, since we hardly had any possessions: some clothes, some shoes, my violin and books, her leotards and dance shoes. We left our cheap pots and pans in a cardboard box on our stoop for someone else to find and hugged each other goodbye, each embarking on an impossible path: her to make a living as a modern dancer, me to study esoteric texts in a language I didn't know, halfway around the world.

I took the bus down to Baltimore for my last week in the States. Mornings, I sat at the dining room table with my mom, eating cereal and talking about the logistics of my trip: traveler's checks, guidebook, phone cards. Afternoons, I borrowed my parents' car and drove down to the cobblestone streets of Fells Point, a maritime neighborhood by the harbor. There I busked for money, playing fiddle tunes with my case open at my feet, a passerby occasionally dropping a dollar onto the dark blue velvet lining.

One day, an old man stopped in front of me. He was eighty years old, and a musician, he said proudly; his name was Lenny. "I play with the Charm City Klezmer Orchestra," he told me, pulling a harmonica out of his pocket. "What about you?"

"I'm just earning some cash before I move to Jerusalem to study for a while," I said. He leaned in a bit. "Are you Jewish?" he asked, and when I nodded, he waved his harmonica near my face. "Play klezmer?"

I shook my head.

"Wait right here," Lenny said, "I have something to give you."

Ten minutes later, he returned with a manila envelope filled with a thick stack of klezmer sheet music. I thanked him and kept playing. Back at my parents' house, I pulled out the folder and started to play through the tunes. A few I recognized as songs my grandmother Sylvia used to sing to me, though I'd almost forgotten them. Humming them, I could see her chunky cloisonné bracelets; her perfume necklace, rose ointment in a small metal locket she wore around her neck like a talisman; her mischievous smile.

I never saw Lenny again, but he was my klezmer angel, giving me my first tunes of the music that would eventually lead me back to New York, and far beyond.

∾

Finally, the date of my flight approached. On my last night at home, I went to an Orioles game with my family, a secular ritual we'd observed throughout my childhood. Cotton candy, orange T-shirts, stadium lights, shouting "O" during the national anthem, riding home on the light rail: now I saw these familiar motions from the outside, as one who would soon be gone. That night, I stuffed T-shirts, pants, and toiletries into my green hiking backpack in my childhood bedroom, and on a hot August morning in 1998, my parents brought me to the airport.

And then I was there. Somehow I found my way to the Haifa shuttle, where I had promised the yeshiva I'd spend a month in ulpan, learning Hebrew at the university to prepare myself. I squeezed into a seat, clutching my backpack between my knees as the small white van pulled out of the airport. The other passengers were quiet.

As we wound our way on the road north to Haifa, I looked out the window at the green hills of the Galilee, where squat apartment buildings were scattered across the hills, clustered together beneath the sky in small clumps. Each building had a flat roof, and on each roof sat five or six white rectangles, propped up diagonally. *Gravestones,* I thought. *So they bury their dead on the roof here.* I imagined the rituals they would carry out on these rooftops, the solemn Hebrew prayers they'd utter.

That's how little I knew about this land: I thought the solar panels were gravestones. Thousands of years of history written by many different people and religions and tribes, a palimpsest etched on these green-dotted hills, and I couldn't read any of it. Who had lived here, whether a hundred years ago or two thousand; if they left, why they left; who could return, and who could not, and why. I didn't even know how to ask. All I knew was that I had left the world I knew.

Part II

Ruth

The story of Ruth is the story of a young woman who reinvents herself almost entirely: moving far from home, transforming her relationships, and shifting her spiritual and cultural beliefs and practices.

She is a Moabite, living in her own land, who has married a foreigner—an Israelite who lives in Moab along with his brother and mother. But he dies, and so does his brother, leaving two women alone: Ruth, and her mother-in-law, Naomi.

Naomi, with no reason to stay in Moab now that her sons have passed away, decides in her grief to return to her native land of Israel. And Ruth, somewhat inexplicably, decides to follow her.

Naomi begs Ruth to stay at home in Moab, in her own land, with her family. But Ruth has made up her mind: *Where you go I will go, and where you stay I will stay. Your people will be my people and your God my God. Where you die I will die, and there I will be buried.*

The book of Ruth can be read as an ode to this young woman's astonishing self-transformation. The risks she chooses to take are not only social and spiritual, but physical; once Ruth and Naomi leave Moab and arrive in the land of Israel, they are destitute and unprotected. They barely survive by gleaning left-behind produce in the fields, and then Naomi has an idea.

During harvest season, knowing that the wealthy landowner (who happens to be a distant cousin) will camp out in his field, Naomi instructs Ruth to crawl into his tent late at night and surprise him. The plan works: Ruth marries him, saving not only herself, but also Naomi, from a life of poverty. And the effects echo over many generations; according to tradition, the son Ruth bears from this marriage eventually leads to the Messiah, who will redeem the entire world.

Ruth's journey takes place in that sweet, early, flying stage of womanhood—no longer a girl, but still young and unencumbered enough to change her life entirely. And yet, as she transforms her life, Ruth does not move in the direction of complete independence. Instead, after claiming her freedom, Ruth uses that freedom to bind herself to Naomi, and to Naomi's tribe.

And Naomi herself? She, too, is on a journey, although she is no longer young. We hear a call, and whenever it comes, we set out. We have to.

Portrait of the Artist as a Kiddush Cup

My first Friday night in Israel, strangers gathered in the hostel's backyard in our best traveling clothes. We stood in a circle as the desk attendant clapped two challahs together and held them in the air. *"Hamotzi lechem min haaretz,"* he chanted, and then continued: "In the name of our Lord Jesus Christ we bless this challah."

Twenty-one years old, I had flown halfway around the world to be with other Jews. I had dreamed of my first Shabbat in Israel, what it would feel like to be in the Holy Land on the holy day. But I had come first to the port town of Haifa, in the north of Israel, to study Hebrew at the University of Haifa. And the only hostel in Haifa was a Christian hostel. So my first Shabbat in Israel was a Christian Shabbat.

In seventh grade, I'd been invited to a Christian youth group by a few friends who belonged to the Presbyterian church. They walked there every Thursday after school to hang out, do crafts, and eat free snacks together; it sounded fun, and I wanted to belong so badly. I begged my parents to let me go; they acquiesced, but they drew the line at my wearing a cross (though I protested, *It's just for fashion!*). When the school bell rang, we'd grab our backpacks, sling them over one shoulder, and walk to the church together, laughing. In the warm camaraderie of the linoleum-floored, wood-paneled church basement, we held hands in a circle during prayer time, while I tried to ignore the dull sense that I was not supposed to be there—that I was in some way lying both to the eager teenager leading the youth group and to myself.

Now I stood on the tiled backyard of a hostel, twenty-one years old, breathing the salt air of the Mediterranean, surrounded by mountains, and my cheeks burned as I answered *Amen.*

And yet the odd truth was that I knew I had something in common with these Christian missionaries on the hostel staff, something that made me different from my family. I, too, was in love with something invisible, and I, too, had traveled far from home to learn about it. *For now I'll say amen to someone else's prayer,* I told myself, *but soon I won't have to. I'll learn to pray. I'll hold the magic tools in my own hands, my own mouth.*

~

On the first day of summer Hebrew classes at the University of Haifa, waiting in line to register, I met an East German student my age. He was blond as a farm boy, a pure Aryan-looking specimen who was apparently—somehow—Jewish. He was a trifecta I found irresistible: intoxicatingly handsome, intrigued by me, and not quite interested. Seeing him, I felt the familiar clench of desire in my stomach, and Zoe flashed through my mind for the first time since I'd left.

When the Berlin Wall fell, he'd been a teenager. But it did not occur to me to ask him how it felt to live through this great moment in modern history; instead, I pursued him with single-minded dedication, like a lion stalking its prey, as we traipsed around Haifa in the hot August afternoons. I was there to learn Hebrew, and

I was in the lowest level, aleph. He was two levels up, in gimel, and his intermediate language skills seemed impossibly capable and sophisticated. Occasionally he would darkly allude to his ex-girlfriend back home in a rehab facility, and it was clear that he was still in love with her, which made him all the more irresistible.

We laughed together, but we also annoyed each other; deep down, I knew that we'd have enjoyed each other for a couple months, at best, before things went sour. But I didn't care. I was alone, with nothing familiar around, memorizing verb conjugations in a lonely dorm room. I wanted a hit of closeness, approval, conquest—I needed it like a drug. And so I chased him.

But toward the end of summer language classes, I finally began to interrogate my desire itself, what it might be covering up. I'd never questioned my all-consuming crushes; like an athlete trying to pull ahead of the front-runner, my vision narrowed, focused entirely on the person I was chasing. It was agonizing, but thrilling, some ancient hunt impulse awakened. Suddenly, I saw it in another light: I was trying to escape my own loneliness by throwing myself into the chase. Wasn't this the opposite of the spiritual discernment I'd come here to seek?

The previous spring, Shira had taught me about the practice of *shomer negiya*—refraining from touching anyone of the opposite sex. No high fives, no handshakes, no brotherly claps on the back. And certainly no soft lips on lips, God forbid, no thumbs bruising thighs, no thrill of beard stubble against neck . . .

If dating was a hamster wheel, maybe *shomer negiya* could be the door out. I could stop touching other people and leave the whole thing behind, like a nun. I imagined myself in long robes, serene. True, I'd have to be careful vis-à-vis the other nuns—but if I could make the right boundary in my mind, I could hold myself apart from any desire, even if *shomer negiya* between the genders left some glaring holes for people like me.

Our university organized a trip to Jerusalem to visit the Wailing Wall, and as we stood in line to board the bus, I felt the habitual instinct to angle for a seat next to the East German. Maybe we'd end up holding hands on the plush bus seat, or I could lean my head on his shoulder on the return trip when the lights were off. But instead, I sat down a couple rows behind him.

I was dressed in schlubby American traveling clothes—purple corduroy pants and a T-shirt with a Roy Lichtenstein print that said *Oh my God, I left the baby on the bus!* But in my mind, I was wrapped in sacred robes as I lowered myself into the seat. I luxuriated in this new feeling of spaciousness, this distance from my own desire, as the bus wound down through the rocky fields and into the narrow streets of Jerusalem.

It was like the moment at the pool when I first realized I could decide not to eat, I thought, except this time I was doing it right, without the shame and self-hatred. This time, rather than trying to fit into some idea of what my body should do, I was stepping aside from my hunger for the right reason: to make space in which I could be more present, less distracted by fleeting desires, more focused on this brief life.

Potiphar's Wife

(Book of Exodus)

On its surface, the story of Potiphar's wife is about unrequited love, a one-way longing that shatters propriety and ends in disaster. But more deeply, this is a story about the complicated, heartbreaking nature of human desire.

Married to a high-up government official, Potiphar's wife is captivated instead by a servant in her home: Joseph, a powerless foreigner. I have compassion for the young, helpless Joseph—recently the victim of insatiable jealousy on the part of his brothers, now the object of maddening lust on the part of his mistress. Potiphar's wife is the one with the power in this household, and she does not use her power for good. When Joseph rebuffs her advances, she lies and accuses him of sexually assaulting her. There's no way around it; she behaves terribly.

And yet I'm fascinated by the fact that a woman's desire is the driving force of this ancient story. And my heart goes out to Potiphar's wife, too.

If she were a man and Joseph a woman, there would hardly be a story here; men of this era could take their servants as concubines without consent. In fact, Joseph's own father, Jacob, had taken his two wives' servants as his third and fourth wives, and Torah does not bother to mention Bilhah and Zilpah's willingness (or lack thereof) to marry their master. And yet here, when Joseph is a servant propositioned by *his* mistress, the text gives Joseph the power to refuse her, even if he'll be put in jail for it.

And refuse he does, a decision the rabbis praise heartily. We might assume Joseph was not interested in her, but some rabbis wonder: Could Joseph have actually reciprocated her desire, and only refused for moral reasons?

The commentators who imagine a turned-on Joseph interpret his refusal as that much more difficult, and therefore more laudable. This is a fun reading, and frankly sexier than the text's plain meaning; but what's their justification within the story itself?

Proponents of this interpretation point to the trope—cantillation melodies for chanting Torah, little squiggles over each word that serve as a form of music notation for those who chant Torah in public. Handed down over the millennia, trope gives us not only the musical notes for chanting, but also interpretive information about Torah verses.

The Hebrew word for "he refused" (Genesis 39:8) is marked with the rare and fabulous *shalshelet* trope mark, which repeats an arpeggiated chord three times. This circular, repeated phrase can sound like a musical representation of certainty—"I won't! I won't! I won't!"—or of hesitation—"Should I? Should I? Should

I?" These commentators interpret the winding, repetitive *shalshelet* trope on the word for "he resisted" as an indication that Joseph had to struggle, not to fend off Potiphar's wife, but to resist his own desire for her.

But I want to return to reading this story through the eyes of Potiphar's wife, her untenable situation as a woman in the throes of desire. Given her actions, it's difficult to imagine her needs being fully met in the context of her marriage. Could she be forgiven, in general, for taking matters into her own hands? If Joseph was indeed interested, maybe she's not such a villain.

Though most Jewish commentaries interpret Potiphar's wife negatively, the Islamic tradition holds a completely different interpretation of her, which also occurs in a medieval Jewish text, Sefer HaYashar. In this version of the story, Potiphar's wife has a name, Zuleika, and she is viewed with compassion—her obsession with Joseph seen as the only possible response to his breathtaking beauty.

At the beginning of the Sefer HaYashar midrash (and throughout earlier Islamic interpretations of this tale), Zuleika's female friends are a sort of stand-in for the reader, bewildered and a bit judgmental about her obsession with Joseph. But Zuleika gives them each a knife and a lemon-like fruit called an etrog, familiar to many Jews as part of the traditional ritual for observing Sukkot, the harvest festival.

Once each woman has her etrog and her knife, Zuleika instructs them to slice the fruit, and arranges for Joseph to walk by at the same time. The women are so mesmerized by Joseph's beauty that they all cut their own palms—without even noticing.

What a compelling scene, an almost 1990s grunge tableau of lust, longing, and cutting. These intense themes—the pain of unrequited love, the tendency toward self-harm, the complicated way that desire can lead to self-destruction—remind me how much of human experience remains consistent across the millennia. By the end of the story, both the women and the reader understand Zuleika's desire as a reasonable response to Joseph's magnificence, holding compassion for Potiphar's wife where before there was judgment.

A Sufi love poem by the great Persian poet Jami retells the story in yet another way, through the prism of sacred love: Yusuf's (Joseph's) beauty represents the beauty of the Divine, the true object of Zuleika's desire. If the biblical story seems to carry a whiff of distaste for Potiphar's wife as a jilted, desirous woman, the song of Zuleika and Yusuf is an ode to her earth-shattering desire to understand and devote herself fully to God's magnificence.

Whichever interpretation we follow, this is a story about the powerful, destabilizing, potentially tragic, potentially liberating force of desire, longing, and lust. A story about the relationship between two forms of desire: our desire for other people, and our desire for God. A story that—like all the best stories—raises more questions than it answers.

The Deer I Did Not See

And then the university bus arrived in Jerusalem after our three-hour journey, and we ungainly foreigners tumbled off, followed our teacher through an ancient gate and then through a warren of stone alleys, and a vista opened up in front of us. The Kotel, the Western Wall.

The Kotel was the retaining wall of the base beneath the ancient Temple, built on a mountain in the center of Jerusalem. The Temple itself was called Beit HaMikdash—the Holy House—and was the beating heart of ancient Jewish ritual. On its stone altar, priests offered sacrifices multiple times a day to reaffirm the connection with the Divine; through its wide gates, Israelite pilgrims streamed three times a year to celebrate the festivals of Passover, Shavuot, and Sukkot; and, according to legend, in its six-branched candelabra, a small vial of oil lasted for eight days: the Chanukah miracle. According to Jewish tradition, this is the most sacred place in the world, and in the Temple's absence, the Western Wall is a place of intense connection with God—as close as we can get.

But I could not feel this holiness as we approached the broad plaza of stone that led to the Wall. In the bright sun, I was sweaty, thirsty, itchy. I had to squeeze aside to avoid the slow-moving tour groups in matching T-shirts, the group leaders with their megaphones, the security guards with their giant guns and dark sunglasses. From far away, the Wall seemed to me like a crude, horizontal version of Notre Dame: impressively old, but not particularly moving.

I was unaware not only of the sacred history, but also of the political layers of this place. I did not realize that approaching this wall as a Jew was one part of a rich and complicated story; that this mountain was holy for Muslims, too; that the sacred Al-Aqsa Mosque now occupied the space where the ancient Temple once stood, and the Israeli government sometimes prevented Muslim pilgrims from accessing their own sacred site.

Later I would consider the injustice of how easily I could enter this space, when others were banned. But I was young, and on my own, just beginning to learn.

And so I approached the Western Wall ignorant of the many invisible layers surrounding me. I approached it the way I would visit any archaeological site in a tourist town: awe at the passage of time, boredom in the face of old stones, and disgust at the way it was all packaged and sold. But when we finally made it to the Wall itself—women on one side, men on the other—I leaned into the cool surface, and my impatience melted away.

I touched my forehead to the massive stone before me. I pressed my lips to it, leaned my entire body against it. I relaxed into it, as if it were a mother, or a lover, or a bed, as if I could finally rest.

And I felt, for the first time, the enormity of Jewish history. I closed my eyes and had a vision of myself as a kiddush cup, a silver vessel, carrying a rare and precious wine. Sweet red wine, dark as blood. My parents had poured it into me, my grandparents into them, and so on all the way back to dim history—continuing this chain improbably, almost impossibly, since the time the Holy Temple stood here.

Through expulsions and excursions and ocean crossings, all the way to my own trembling twenty-one-year-old American body, standing there in my purple corduroy pants. I had carried something magical all these years. I had been called here to learn this magic, to taste the wine, to become a better vessel, to keep it safe so that one day I could pour it into my own children, they into theirs.

My sobs caught me by surprise. Small and quiet, they jerked up from my belly, convulsing my solar plexus, pulling my shoulders forward. I wept into the cold, huge, rough-hewn stones, and against its massive weight, my body relaxed. I felt myself disappear—my name, my family, my stories, gone. Absorbed into the enormity of stone.

What relief it was, to let go of these incidental details about my existence. To release my childhood bedroom and the suburbs and Cabbage Patch Kids and speaking English and microwave lasagna and grades and Greyhound buses and my hopes and dreams for the future. To think I could have been born anywhere, anytime, as a Jew, and I might have found my way to this stone wall. All the facts of my own life suddenly temporary, a conduit, a container for something magical that would pass through me and be given to someone else to carry.

My tears streaked the stone, dirty on my cheeks. I walked away, taking careful steps backward so as not to turn my back on the holy wall, and an old woman took my place and began whispering into the stone where I had just stood.

∾

Back in Haifa for the last couple weeks of ulpan, no longer chasing the East German boy, I began to spend my lunch breaks playing violin in the woods behind the university. Each morning, the security guards at the school's entrance eyed my rectangular case suspiciously as I carried it through the metal detector. It had never occurred to me someone might think my violin case contained a gun, or how permeable the membranes of space were in late 1990s America: no armed guards at the mall, no metal detectors at university. Here, there was a faint overlay of violence and security. I tasted its metallic tinge, its intertwined aura of threat and protection.

In the woods behind the university cafeteria, language faded. There was only silence, and trees, and the music I played. I opened my case, cradled my instrument, took out the bow, tightened the hair; it felt like a wand. I played the slow waltzes I'd learned on the street in New York, the Yiddish songs my grandmother used to sing, for an audience of cedars.

One day, a friend from New York appeared in the cafeteria at lunchtime like a messenger from another life. He was backpacking through Israel and a friend had told him I was studying at the University of Haifa, so he'd come to see if he could find me. We bought tuna sandwiches and I took him to the clearing, where I played while he sat on a rock beside me. "Did you see those deer?" he asked me as we walked back. "They were so beautiful."

I had not seen any deer. My eyes were closed. "They came out of the woods while you were playing," he said, "and they stood around you in a circle, listening."

There was so much I did not see, did not understand, and only one week until yeshiva began.

A Sky-Blue Room

The yeshiva was sunny and homey, and smelled of coffee and books and fresh air. I exhaled with relief, looking around the space on my first day. September 1999. Students lounged on couches in a large, central room filled with cafeteria-style tables. Surrounding this communal space: cozy classrooms, a kitchen, and just down the hall, a large, bright library where students were beginning to gather. A tall man in a knitted kippah motioned me toward the library. "Welcome, welcome! Come on in to the *beit midrash*!" I'd taken the bus that morning from a hostel in the old city, where I was staying in a room with six bunk beds, and I felt overwhelmed with newness, a rush of unfamiliar faces and names and something deeper, too, ground shifting beneath my feet.

The yeshiva was primarily for English speakers, so though I was dizzyingly far from home, at least I understood what everyone was saying; the day passed in a school-like routine of classes, discussion, and textbooks, with occasional Hebrew words I struggled to decipher. But as soon as the school day ended, anxiety descended on me. I spoke neither the language of this country, nor the language of the religious rituals that surrounded me, and I couldn't stay in the communal bunk room at the hostel all year.

On the third day, at lunchtime, I sat with the other students at long cafeteria tables. The room was buzzing with conversation as we served ourselves from large disposable aluminum trays of tabouleh, hummus, and falafel. I gathered my courage and forced myself to stand up. I waved nervously. “Uh, hi everyone . . . I just wanted to say, I need a place to live, if anyone has an open room.”

Though the room was large, the person who raised her hand sat directly across the table from me. Her brown eyes sparkled beneath a mop of curly brown hair, and gold thread wove through the bright orange scarf woven loosely around her neck. “I do!” she said.

A brief smattering of applause from my fellow students. “Oh wow! Great!” I smiled and sat back down.

I moved in with Emily that night, lugging my big green backpack up to the third floor. I slept on the cold tile floor of my new room, overjoyed to have a home. Within two weeks, we were best friends. One day in class, we learned about the mystical significance of the sacred blue, a turquoise shade called *techelet.* It symbolized the throne of God, the sky, the sea. I bought a can of sky-blue paint and covered the walls of my bedroom.

Emily suggested we host a Shabbat dinner. Though I didn’t know the prayers, and had never hosted any sort of dinner party, she had already lived on a kibbutz for a year and knew how to do such things. We were quickly becoming friends with our fellow students, and soon we had eight guests arriving in our little apartment. We didn’t have a living room, so we turned my mattress on its side to make more space and ate cross-legged on the hard, gray-colored tiles of my bedroom, laughter and singing echoing off the walls, surrounded by sacred blue, as if we were in the sky.

∾

Familiar school-rhythms took hold: my "aleph level" classmates and I joked, studied verb conjugations, began to unravel the arcane rules of ancient sacrifices, which used to happen regularly a few miles away at the Beit HaMikdash but had not been performed for two thousand years. We were the lowest level, and, unlike the other students, we used side-by-side translations as we painstakingly learned to decode the ancient texts. Along with the basics of biblical Hebrew, we surreptitiously studied the people who had grown up religious, or had been in yeshiva long enough to act that way—it was hard to tell the difference. Long skirts for the women, yarmulkes for men, a smattering of Yiddish words among the English, holy books in Aramaic tucked beneath arms, as they might have been five hundred years ago (except that women carried them too).

We all gathered to pray three times a day: morning, afternoon, evening. Three times a day, I stumbled over the words. I snuck envious glances from behind my siddur, looking with longing at the students who chanted so fluently, as if prayer were easy. I wished there were a magic pill I could take to ingest their knowledge, to build a night sky of constellations inside my mind: when to bow, when to take three steps back, when to whisper silently, eyes closed, holding my siddur to my lips.

"You don't need to recite the blessing for bread before eating pita," a seven-year-old Orthodox boy told me at a Shabbat lunch at his house. "It's not really bread." It did not occur to me to question his teaching; he was seven, but he had grown up his whole life in this tradition I was just entering. For three weeks after that, I did not recite the bread blessing before eating pita, until I found out that he was entirely mistaken. Pita is indisputably bread; the word "pita" may derive from *pat*, which appears in Proverbs 17:1:

> *Better a crust of bread* [pat] *with peace*
> *Than a house full of feasting with strife.*

~

I was part of a group now, and I delighted in the simple fact of being in community: our caring for each other, our mutual acceptance, our openhearted invitations. I knew where I'd be and who I'd be with every day of the week, and it was a relief. Sunday through Thursday, we were at school; on Shabbat, Emily and I either hosted or walked to someone's house for Friday night dinner, someone else's for Saturday lunch, and another for "third meal," the smaller meal late Saturday afternoon.

By the time each meal started, we'd walked to synagogue, prayed for hours, and walked to the host's apartment. I was always ravenous, but before the meal could begin, we recited a series of prayers. First the host chanted the kiddush blessing, tipped the silver cup to their lips, and drank a few swallows of wine. Then we filed to the sink, placed our rings on the counter, washed our fingers with the two-handled ritual vessel, and refilled the vessel with cold water for the next person. Finally, we recited the handwashing prayer as we dried our hands, handed the towel to the next person, and slid our rings back on.

Since the handwashing was a ritual purification to prepare us for bread, as the ancient priests once did in the Temple, we did not speak between the handwashing blessing and the bread blessing. Instead, we sang wordless songs, clapping and banging on the table. Then the host removed the cloth covering the challah, chanted the *hamotzi* blessing, tore off small pieces of challah, dipped them in salt, and either put them on a plate to pass around or tossed them high in the air toward each of us—symbolically acknowledging that bread comes not from humans, but from God.

By then, my stomach would be twitching painfully, my eager salivary glands kicking into anticipation. Bowls of *salatim* were passed around the table—baba ghanoush, store-bought with whipped eggplant, and hummus, creamy and tangy. Then came the loaf of challah, from which we each tore a warm braid-bump before passing it along. We used the challah chunk in our hands to scoop the creamy *salatim,* all on the beige spectrum but adorned with roasted red peppers, olive oil, zataar spices, or toasted pine nuts. Meanwhile, whoever was hosting hurried back and forth, helped by whoever was sitting closest to the door: table to kitchen, kitchen to table, bearing heaping bowls of paprika chicken or pasta salad or marinated tofu.

The baba ghanoush was soft, slightly sweet, with a nutty flavor. Each challah-scooped tablespoon tasted like floating on a pale eggplant cloud. It was comfort food, like home against my tongue: not the home of my childhood, but a new one. I knew the blessings now, when to be silent and when to speak. My body grew softer.

~

My parents had given me an 800 number that would allow me to call them and put the international charges on their phone bill, and every couple weeks I phoned to say hello. Remembering my previous life was like looking out a spaceship's porthole at the earth, only the barest thread of these phone calls connecting me. College felt like a distant dream. But a few weeks after yeshiva began, Shira emailed me. *I'm passing through in a few weeks, visiting friends,* she wrote, and I remembered that she'd mentioned this trip when we'd said goodbye. *Do you want to get coffee?* I smiled, remembering that while I felt like an astronaut in this new life, for Shira it was all normal.

We met at an outdoor café downtown. I rarely went anywhere except yeshiva and had trouble with basic Hebrew, but Shira navigated with comfort. She was wearing a T-shirt that ended just above her elbows, revealing her previously covered forearms, and her usual seriousness had been replaced with a flurry of blushes and giggles. When we sat down with our coffees, she motioned for me to come closer and whispered, her eyes lit like moons, that she had kissed a soldier named Moshe. She showed me a picture of him. He had light hair like her—that Russian Jewish red hair the Israelis call *gingi*—a knitted yarmulke on his head, and a cocky smile.

It took a while for me to realize what was going on: This was her first kiss. Shira was changing, too. I never saw her again, but in that moment, I felt we finally understood each other.

Nehemiah's Song

A dream is one-sixtieth of prophecy, the Talmud says, and sleep is one-sixtieth of death. And if a drop of dairy falls into a pot of meat soup, it is still kosher, as long as the dairy is less than one-sixtieth of the total volume of the soup. *Batel b'shishim,* nullified by the rule of sixty: Less than one-sixtieth is counted as if it does not exist.

After four months in Jerusalem, something suddenly tipped over. The strangers I sat beside each day had become my friends; now the texts came alive. Before, each word had entered my brain slowly, through a painstaking screen of translation. Now I could ingest them directly, and they moved through me quickly, changing me. I felt sparks, as if my mind might catch fire.

Numbers are ideas as much as quantities: Seven is a single cycle of natural completion. Eight: one step beyond the cycle, supernatural. Forty: a full cycle, a generation, an incarnation. And letters are numbers, too. In gematria, each letter has its value. Aleph is one, tav four hundred. "Wine" adds up to seventy, as does "secret," and so when the Talmud says "In goes wine, out goes secret," it is both a timeless truth and a math joke. On Purim, when we are commanded to drink until we do not know the difference between "cursed be Haman" and "blessed be Mordechai," the letters of which add up to the same number, this commandment is a radical proposal of a space beyond right and wrong—and also a math joke.

"Heart" is thirty-two; I would use this number in PINs and passwords for decades to come.

"Life" is eighteen, the one that made it through the pinhole of American culture to even my watered-down bat mitzvah, garnering me checks in multiples of eighteen tucked into Hallmark cards from my great-aunts and -uncles.

Like a secret message they didn't realize they were passing on: *Don't forget me. One day, when you're ready, come back and find out what this all means.* And finally I had. I returned to these books for the first time.

What I found there: Miniature scrolls on doorposts, braided candles and spice boxes. Fingertips touched to books, then lightly kissed. Whispered Hebrew prayers, consonants notching the out-breath; Torah chanting and its plaintive, brave, matter-of-fact melodies: Yemenite, Ashkenazi, Sephardi. The space between bodies sensed more strongly for not touching; braided loaves rising in the oven. Dresses, headscarves, kippot and prayer shawls; electric boundary where the sacred touches the everyday. Baba ghanoush, *melafafonim.* The prayers my great-great-great-great-great-great-grandparents had chanted long ago, when Grandma Lee and Grandpa Dick and Grandma Sylvia and Grandpa Al were a distant dream of the future. The desert; light on white stone.

∾

At the same time the language began to click for me, I fell in love with the rules.

The eros of spiritual practice: dos and don'ts, will and won't, forbidden and permitted.

Shomer negiya had been an experiment on the bus from Haifa six months ago; now it was a practice. The whispered sense of lines just barely touching my body, brushing against the nipples of the soul, if there were such a thing, some extra-sensitive apparatus, a darker pink that quivers to attention when it feels itself grazed by the sacred. That old love of asceticism, of restraint, of boundaries—now pointed toward life, not death. The violin part of my brain lit up: the quiet attention of hours alone in a practice room, the simple pleasure of working toward a goal which shut out all other goals, the rush of orchestral gratitude as my own sound merged with others' to create something greater.

The hair on my forearms stood up as I walked through Jerusalem not touching men, pausing wherever I was at the hour for prayers, not eating dairy within six hours after eating meat. I mouthed the morning *tefila* on the public bus to the yeshiva, standing beside a pole, rocking back and forth with my tiny siddur. I closed my eyes as I whispered bedtime prayers in my room, facing east to the ancient Temple, where the Divine is said to touch the earth, an hour's walk from the apartment I shared with Emily.

Living inside these rules, I felt my skin as a screen, an interface with the world. I was conscious of existing in the medium of time, on which being paints itself every second anew. I stood in a labyrinth of invisible force fields, positive and negative ions, atoms made into the size of planets, planets collapsed to the size of marbles.

Had I grown up inside this system, I'm certain it would be stifling, and I would need to break the rules to release the energy stored in them—as later I would dismantle them one by one, with the same intuitive groping in the dark that led me here to learn them.

But I did not grow up in these rules. To me, they were not restrictive; instead, they were esoteric, radical, contraband. They liberated me from everything I did not like about myself, from my uncertainty about where I stopped and the world began, the feeling of overflowing my boundaries. They freed me from the drudgery of infinite small choices, the burden of meaning-making, the alienating loneliness of being twenty-one, a young woman with no idea what she was going to do with her life, who knew nonetheless that she needed to change it. They assuaged my hunger for intimacy, my longing to be close to other people, other lives, to be part of a tribe: not just with the Jews who happened to be alive at the moment, but with those beyond the wall of time. Humans, in their bodies, their costumes, made more human to me by the distance between our centuries and the similarities of our shared, mysterious destiny.

∾

Every Friday night, the yeshiva students gathered in one of our apartments to eat dinner and sing *zemirot,* Shabbat table songs, late into the night. At one friend's apartment, an old woman lived directly below him, and would bang on her ceiling with a broom as we sang. I was mystified: Who would not want to hear this chorus of praise? So what if it was ten p.m.?

To read the words of the songs, which were all in Hebrew or Aramaic, we used miniature Shabbat songbooks. They were stained with wine and food and crumbs; whoever was hosting would pass them out after the main course, and collect them with the dishes at the end of the night, after we had chanted the Birkat HaMazon, the grace after meals. These little books were called *bentschers,* from the Yiddish word for "bless," and they were given to guests as wedding favors; each had the name of a different couple on the front. I'd trace the names with my finger, dreaming of giving out *bentschers* to the guests at my own wedding.

We sang biblical psalms. We sang *niggunim,* Hasidic songs without words, syllables that even the most recently arrived neophyte could join in: *Yai dai dai, yai da dai dai.* We sang songs in praise of Shabbat written in rhymed medieval Hebrew, and when I glanced over to the English side of the page, I could barely make sense of the antiquated lyrics, but the meaning lay in the melodies, our voices becoming one. We sang in Hebrew of fish and waffles, honey and blessings, giving thanks to God as *a tower from whom we have eaten.*

Choosing the next song was always an informal process. There would be a silence, then, "Do you guys know that Yemenite version of Yom Zeh L'Yisrael?" someone would ask, and off we'd go. It was the closest life could get to a musical, breaking into song in the middle of dinner.

My favorite melodies, from North African or Middle Eastern communities, wore the scales and rhythms of that part of the world. Equally beautiful were the Hasidic melodies from Eastern Europe. I was less fond of the ones that sounded like German drinking songs, and I rolled my eyes at the psalms sung to Beach Boys melodies and Beatles tunes and cheery camp songs punctuated by hand-claps. These tunes were nostalgic for the people who, unlike me, grew up going to Jewish summer camp. Lacking those memories, I groaned each time someone suggested one of the new songs; I hadn't come halfway across the world to sing ancient Hebrew words to pop songs.

But there was one new song I loved. Someone named Nehemiah had written it, so everyone called it "Nehemiah's Song." A sweet name, Nehemiah: *God consoles.* At first the melody sounded simple: a minor key, a few steps down, then back up. But there was magic in its six notes. After a few repetitions, the room would begin to glow a bit, the music breathing and swelling in our bodies. People would begin to close their eyes and sing louder; we'd push our chairs back from the table, everything but the music blurring, as we let the melody overtake us with its wordless yearning.

I, too, occasionally would write a new melody and teach it to some friends. They were kind enough to sing it for a few weeks, but my melodies never caught on, and I was secretly jealous of this Nehemiah whose simple song had spread across the entire English-speaking community of Jerusalem. What did he know that I didn't?

No More Temporary Unions

A few weeks after we'd moved in together, Emily had taken me to the cheap store near the *shuk* so we could buy cheap flowing cotton hippie dresses embroidered with curving patterns, to observe the tradition of wearing something new for Rosh Hashanah: the New Year. In our circles, synagogue fashion overlapped closely with the Dead show parking lots of my youth; I thought of myself at fourteen, wandering on the asphalt, looking for something. Emily knew which synagogues we should choose from for each service of Rosh Hashanah—which had women chanting Torah as well as men; which promised the best *drash,* or sermon; which the most *ruach,* or spirit.

The holiday lasts two nights and two days (as I'd learned at Shira's the year before)—and after each service someone, usually in their forties or fifties, old enough to be established and with enough money to afford to feed a big group, would stand up. "Hi, everyone," they'd say, "we're hosting a meal. If anyone doesn't have a place to be, just follow me and join us at our house."

I'd never experienced that kind of hospitality before, except (again) in the parking lot before Dead shows. Otherwise, even in the most tightly knit scenes I'd been a part of, there were layers of in and out, complicated negotiations of allegiance and pride, newcomers and old guard. This felt like an ancient hospitality I'd stepped into, and I never wanted to leave. How, I wondered, had I been lucky enough to find myself here?

The second morning of Rosh Hashanah, the person to stand up and invite stragglers into his house was a kind-looking man named Chayim, an American living in Jerusalem. He was short, with graying hair and crinkly eyes that reminded me of my father. I walked over and introduced myself, and he was clearly delighted to be taken up on his offer. "Wonderful," he said, "my wife's just over there, we'll all be leaving soon, just follow us!"

Chayim seemed to be a good, gentle man—intelligent, with a sense of humor. Suddenly I missed my dad painfully. Our calling-card conversations were warm, my parents passing the phone back and forth to say hello, and I could feel them begin to relax as they heard me remain essentially myself, rather than (as they feared) getting sucked into a Jewish cult.

Not a cult, but still foreign to the way I'd been raised: I was becoming part of this community of seekers who had made a new home. I had begun to get my bearings enough to know that Chayim did not grow up with that name. Like me, he had traveled far to find his place here, and an image flashed in my mind: me, one day in the future, hosting some young wanderer at my own Rosh Hashanah meal.

As we left the synagogue and walked to their apartment, Chayim and his kind, short-haired wife gathered a group—a few stragglers like me, others longtime friends of the family who had already planned to attend their lunch. Together we made our way down the street, savoring the sun after hours in the synagogue. Their house was just a few blocks from my apartment, but unlike my bare floor with a blanket and my backpack, theirs was filled with the comfortable items of a family who had lived there for decades. Pictures of their kids, who seemed to be around my age; textiles from travels around the Middle East; and the omnipresent sacred books lined up on the shelf, as always, calling to me.

I expected to stay silent and watch these old friends chat, but it turned out people at lunch were interested in the stories of young seekers like me as we perched, ill at ease, on Chayim's comfortable sofas, fingering the Egyptian textiles that covered them. I remembered last Rosh Hashanah, when Shira's family treated me with the same curiosity and kindness: *Where are you from? How long have you been here? What kind of community did you grow up in? What did you study in school?* I listened to myself answer and felt how strongly my life was in flux, how I was a stranger not only to this place but to myself. Perhaps this journey was about taking myself apart piece by piece, and seeing what grew out of the empty space at the center of me. Maybe it was understandable that my parents had been so worried.

It came out, through questioning, that I played the violin and knew some fiddle tunes. Hearing this, someone waved Chayim over—he, too, loved bluegrass, and was part of a folk music society that hosted concerts and jam sessions. And like that, Chayim and I became friends. He took me under his wing, driving me to the bluegrass events out of town. He kept tabs on my Torah studies, as proud as if I were his own daughter. He even set up a small performance for me in Tel Aviv. Sometimes he would drop by the yeshiva to give a class or study on his own; I was always glad to see him in the hallways, where we greeted each other as beloved friends.

Over the months, as my Hebrew skills grew and my Torah study deepened, Chayim began to mentor me more actively. "I see something in you," he said, "something of myself." On the drive to concerts and jam sessions, he asked about the texts I was studying in my classes. He challenged my interpretations, suggested alternate translations of the Hebrew words, brought in rabbinic commentary from other texts. This was how teachers showed respect to students, I understood, and my mind arched and grew in response, shooting up, incorporating new words, new concepts, spreading from one to the next like the kudzu that covers vegetation in the land those fiddle tunes came from.

~

As fall turned to winter, I began to understand more about this world I'd entered; ideas and assumptions that had been invisible to me came into focus. Marriage, for example. I'd always thought of it as an abstract, boringly adult convention. Here, marriage was the goal, the purpose, the end of the story toward which all stories tended. The point, the resolution, the loose ends of life tied into a neat bow complete with a package of photos—then a baby, then two or three more.

Everyone, it seemed, was either married, engaged, or dating—and not dating for fun, but deadly serious, on their way to engagement. The engaged couples did not live together, but they glowed as they cohosted Shabbat lunches, slow-danced at other couples' weddings, and arrived a little late to shul together on Saturday morning.

I understood this longing for ballast, binding, this desire to hold together the entropic energy of life. No more temporary unions, flimsy as plastic. Not passion, so sweet and deep and yet fleeting; not longing, that sharp, hungry edge of desire. Marriage would be, instead, like the ancient stone mikvahs that had withstood two thousand years, still standing beneath the ruins of entire civilizations. A partnership: stable, rich, complex yet simple, providing container and shape, sanction and the imprimatur of adulthood.

At twenty-one, according to the unspoken timeline of this

community, I still had a few years left to find my *bashert*—my soulmate—without too much concern. But Emily, at twenty-seven, felt her singleness acutely. She was looking for a husband, and with only three years before she turned thirty, her single status was tinged with worry.

Part of me knew this should feel appalling—that there was more to life than marriage—but it also felt exhilarating. Sex, loneliness, and the longing to belong; they all funneled so beautifully into the receptacle of marriage. Plus, I had always felt older than I was, so it was a relief to find out I was right: I *was* older than I was. Life moved faster here. Youth ended earlier.

I thought about Wednesday Night Learning, back in the distantly remembered universe of America. Now I understood why Shira asked if people on a date had sex right away. The rules of dating in college had seemed so obvious to me, but they were just as invisible as the rules here. My knowledge of how and when to kiss or be kissed was no different from the way everyone in Jerusalem knew which blessing to whisper when, which objects you could touch on Shabbat and which were *muktzeh*.

But I was crossing between worlds now. I had not kissed anyone in five months, had barely thought about it. Once, a fellow yeshiva student asked me on a date. The truth was, I'd noticed him immediately when I arrived; I felt a strong pull toward him, and the year before, I would have accepted enthusiastically, thinking myself quite adult for going on a date rather than relying on the usual wordless assessment that we both wanted to make out. But now I knew immediately that although I had a bit of a crush on him, I didn't want to marry him. And he wasn't asking if I wanted to hook up; he was asking if I wanted to start the process of seeing if we should spend our lives together.

What a relief it was to simply say, *You're so great, but I don't think we're meant for each other*, and mean it. There was no awkwardness the next morning; if anything, we were even more comfortable in our friendship than before. We had played our parts well, and we knew it.

I felt myself losing my taste for my old world, beginning to forget the rules of when to call, how far to go, how hard to chase. And crossing over, instead, to this place, where men and women did not touch, even to shake hands. It was a relief to keep our bodies separate, a relief to lose the threat that had always accompanied men's touches, which I had never quite understood until this place, where a man and a woman did not even ride alone in an elevator. Where, when my Bible teacher wanted to demonstrate that something I'd said was sweet, he pinched his own cheek instead of touching mine.

When a student did get engaged, we closed the sacred books and gathered in the common space to sing and dance in circles until our legs and voices were exhausted—to announce that this was the pinnacle of holiness, the big finale, the reason we had traveled so far to be here.

~

Once in a while, as the months passed, Chayim would say something that struck me as odd. I could never quite identify it; not sexual innuendo, exactly, but his cheerleading occasionally crossed the line into something that felt inappropriate, grandiose, and my danger antennas quivered.

He told me how fast I learned, how much he loved my violin playing; he predicted great things for me. I responded by asking how he met his wife. He brought me literature about study retreats, began to hint we might attend one together. I asked about his daughter, my age and living in America—what was she like?

It took a while to stop thinking of Chayim as an analog to my father. It took a while, also, to realize that I, who felt close to invisible with my baggy skirts and clumsy Hebrew skills, could be an object of . . . desire? pursuit? by a married middle-aged man with children my age, a member of this beautiful community with God at the center, a man who loved our tradition, who devoted himself to the texts not as a fundamentalist might but as a thinking adult who had chosen this life and wanted to share it with others. A man who opened his home to strangers on Rosh Hashanah.

I appreciated the attention. I liked feeling visible. But I'd shifted from feeling seen to feeling threatened, and I no longer felt like a mentee; I felt like prey.

Once that shift happened, my life changed. A thin shadow of fear lay over everything. Sometimes, on my walk home from the yeshiva, Chayim would pop out from around a corner. "I thought I might find you here," he'd say, his face alight with joy. I'd nervously smile and shiver as he walked me the rest of the way home, chatting happily, inviting me to Shabbat dinner, to jam sessions, to fancy lectures on the other side of town.

As the weeks went on, I began to find notes slipped beneath my apartment door, scribbled on torn-off notebook paper. One suggested a book I might like, another had the name of a new bluegrass album. Sometimes these notes praised me: my learning, my violin playing. They seemed innocent, but then why did they frighten me so much?

I didn't know what to do, so I pretended not to understand what was happening. I smiled, nodded, demurred, excused myself politely. Meanwhile, Chayim's notes grew bolder, finally crossing over into confessions of desire. Tuesday: *I've never felt this way before, not even in my twenty-five years of marriage.* Thursday: *I know we're meant to be together.* Friday: *You're driving me crazy.*

I had no idea what to do. I'd been there a couple seasons; he'd lived there twenty years. He seemed to be friends with all my teachers. What would I say, and to whom? And wasn't I, in some way, responsible? I accepted his mentorship, his rides to Tel Aviv, his Torah lessons; I benefited from his interest; it felt good to have the attention, so I allowed it to continue. I had been naïve to think that being married, with a daughter my age, meant he was safe. I should have understood the danger earlier and walked away. I should not have trusted him just because he reminded me of my father.

I decided I would not tell anyone. I would just ignore him until he went away. I hid my face and turned back to the texts. Surely they would hold some answers for me.

All the Healing Waters in the World

"The world is broken," our Bible teacher told us, "but it can be healed." In fact, fixing, healing, repairing, is one of our great human imperatives. In Hebrew: *tikkun.*

I began to wonder, What inside me could be healed? The last people I would have expected to understand my fraught relationship with my body, my complicated history with food, were the Hasidic masters. But then I began to read them: *To eat is to raise trapped sparks of Divine energy that lie inside the food. In eating, then performing good deeds with the energy we take from the food, we liberate those sparks, and send them back to their infinite source.*

Food is magical, fraught, on the border of life and death. It can nourish, it can damage; its absence can kill us, its presence can heal us. And the very fact of living in a body is a complex and ever-changing negotiation between miracle and challenge, power and powerlessness. It was understandable to wrestle with embodiment, and it was also possible to heal, more deeply than I had imagined.

And what about the balance between restriction and permission? Following every single impulse I felt was a trap, but so was overly denying myself. *The right side of the body is compassion; the left side, judgment. Each contains the other, and we strive to balance them, but always to lean slightly towards the side of compassion. For this reason, we always put the right shoe on first.*

I felt at home, surrounded by people who were also devoted to the invisible. As if that childhood magic finally revealed itself clearly, not just to me but to everyone around me, as we bowed in prayer, kissed stones, and bent our heads over the Talmud, sounding out ancient Aramaic words from that quilt of letters spread on the tables before us.

At what time may you begin to recite the morning Shema? When there is enough light to distinguish between sky blue and white. But Rabbi Eliezer says you have to wait until you can distinguish between blue and green.

These micro-distinctions themselves felt healing—liberating me from my personal story, with its excruciating individuality, and gathering me instead to a world outside me. Freed of the burden of living alone with magic.

If this was possible, could I heal the part of Grandma Lee that lived inside me, too? Could I trace that anxiety back through the generations and perform a *tikkun* on each one, repairing the path anxiety had traveled down to her, and to me?

If a person holds a rodent in his hand, even if he immerses in all the healing waters in the world, his immersion is ineffective. But if he casts it from his hand—once he immerses in the mikvah, he is pure.

Through the rabbis' eyes I paid attention to the present moment for the first time: the sharp tang of sunset, the pale cream of early morning. I stood alone in the *beit midrash* library after dark and felt the texts vibrating with their neon wisdom, the years of human energy poured into thick books. The black at the center of the rabbis' eyes was the black of the ink, a direct conduit into their souls, and I took this black ink into my own pupils now. The rabbis were Egyptian, French, Babylonian, Russian. They were ancient, medieval, modern. These nationalities and eras were nothing more than flavors of experience, as I now understood *American, born 1977,* to be my flavor, not my essence. Beneath that, we were brothers, sisters, siblings, family, connected by this web of letters.

~

Inside the walls of the yeshiva, I threw myself into my studies and forgot about Chayim. But when I left, the sense of threat rushed back in; I shivered walking home from yeshiva, and didn't relax until class started the next morning. What had been a vague worry grew into actual fear; everything was turning ominous, my whole world colored by threat. I felt like the sky was dark, as if someone had put a giant hand above my head, but it was balmy out; the cloud was Chayim, in my head now, covering up the sun. I finally decided I had to tell someone. I gathered the letters he slipped under my door, stuffed them into a manila envelope, and brought them with me on the next yeshiva field trip.

On the four-hour bus ride to the desert hike, spirits were high. All around me students joked in the heat, sipping from water bottles, crunching on peanut-butter-flavored Bamba snacks in their crinkly wrappers, the landscape a tan blur outside the window. Trembling, I walked up the aisle to the front of the bus, supporting myself on the seatbacks as the vehicle rocked from side to side. At the front, my Bible teacher sat with the other instructors. He was Chayim's age, maybe fifty years old, and I was pretty sure they were friends. I didn't know how he would respond to this. But I had no choice.

"Um, excuse me? Can I talk to you for a minute, alone?" He looked up, surprised, but also smiling. He was a kind and generous soul who worked on the front lines of spirituality, teaching the aleph class students with the least Jewish knowledge; he was used to questions coming from the seekers who were always showing up at the yeshiva to find themselves.

He gestured for me to sit down beside him, scooting over so our bodies wouldn't touch, and I stuttered the story out in a few abrupt sentences. "I don't know what's going on but something weird is happening. Here—here are the letters."

My teacher's smile disappeared as he took a deep breath. "Okay. Stay here. Let me talk to the dean for a minute. Can I keep these?"

He pushed up to his feet and walked a couple rows back, where he sat down next to the dean. I picked at my cuticles, trembling. Would they chastise me for my part in this sordid story? Ask what I did to give him this impression that we were having a relationship? Kick me out? Tell me Chayim was harmless, a respected member of the community, and not to worry? I couldn't stay here any longer if they said that; was this the end of my time in Jerusalem?

Ten minutes later, my teacher returned with the dean, both of them lumbering down the aisle as the bus swayed side to side through the Judaean desert. They sat down beside me, their faces serious.

"Alicia, we want you to know we take this very seriously. We will speak to Chayim as soon as we get back to Jerusalem. He will no longer be welcome at the yeshiva, and he is to stay away from you off campus, too. If you even see him on the street, you should let us know immediately. On the other hand, there is a mitzvah of not causing public embarrassment when possible. So we want to take care of this as privately as possible. Does this sound okay to you? Would you mind not discussing this with others?"

I did not take it for granted that my teachers chose to believe me, and to protect me.

At the same time, I would later learn that this principle of not causing public embarrassment is used by some ultra-Orthodox rabbis to protect men who abuse their wives. The dangerous side of this law—this entire system, in fact, this labyrinth of sacredness, ethics, and magic—is that it can be used as a tool of oppression. Against women, queer people, anyone with less power.

I saw Chayim again only once, years later, in a crowded synagogue in New York. My chest seized and I looked away, panicked. When I looked back, he was gone.

Serakh bat Asher

(Book of Genesis, Book of Numbers, Midrash)

She is only briefly mentioned in the Torah. But in rabbinic legends, Serakh bat Asher expands to magical proportions; in a world of men, she becomes something of a quiet superhero.

In these legends, Serakh has a range of connected powers, both creative and spiritual. She is a singer-songwriter who uses music to carry out a delicate, pastoral task; a wise woman who knows her people's history intimately; a mystical character who possesses the ability to transcend death; and a holder of cultural memory who knows more than the rabbis themselves.

Her first extraordinary moment comes when she is a girl, or perhaps a teenager—and, despite her youth, the only one who can save her grandfather. Earlier in Genesis, Joseph's brothers, jealous of his status as favored son, throw him into a pit and leave him for dead. One of these brothers is Asher, Serakh's father.

When the brothers return to their father, they lie about what happened to Joseph, saying, "Your beloved son has been killed by a wild animal." In fact, though, Joseph has been bought by slave traders and sold in Egypt.

Years pass, during which Joseph's brothers live their lives, and their father assumes his favorite son is dead. Then a famine hits the region. Joseph's brothers travel to Egypt, to beg for food from the storehouses there. They're received by none other than Joseph—who is not only alive and well, but has risen to become Pharaoh's right-hand man.

Here's where Serakh comes in. Joseph reconciles with his brothers, and invites his extended family to move down to Egypt so that he can provide for them—but there is a problem. Their elderly father, back in Canaan, has long believed his favorite son to be dead. How can the brothers reveal the news that Joseph lives, without giving their father a shock that will kill him?

This situation cannot be solved with muscle; the superpowers needed are empathy, creativity, and nuance. And Serakh possesses these qualities. She is a songwriter and a singer, and these skills give her the ability to save her grandfather's life by delivering the information through art. She builds a song-shaped container to hold the news that Joseph is alive—and also to hold her grandfather's grief and joy, so that it will not break his body.

Reading about Serakh, I think about the close relationship between art-making, healing, prayer, and song. We are taught to separate these practices entirely: "religion" and "art," "therapy" and "creativity," "healing" and "music." These paths, we're told, require entirely different training: music conservatory (or art school, or theater school, or film school) versus rabbinical school (or seminary, or other spiritual training programs).

But are they really so different? All of these paths, whether we call them "artistic" or "spiritual," create a container, a sacred space—a brief respite from everyday life, in which we humans, so often overwhelmed with the details of getting through the day, can experience a sense of holiness and connectedness to ourselves and each other. Perhaps Serakh's song exists as a beautiful symbol of this profound kinship between art and spirituality, music and healing.

Serakh's story does not end here. In fact, according to rabbinic legend, it never ends. When her grandfather hears her sing, he understands that she has performed a miracle for him, and in exchange he blesses her with eternal life.

Her immortality enables her to become an oracle for her people, holding cultural memory across generations. Hundreds of years later, Serakh will remember the location where Joseph's bones were buried beneath the Nile—crucial information, since Joseph's descendants, having previously promised to take his bones back to the Land of Israel, could not leave Egypt without them.

Many generations later, the midrash tells a story about Serakh visiting the rabbis in the *beit midrash*. They're debating the technicalities of how exactly the waters parted to allow the Exodus from Egypt when Serakh suddenly appears to set them straight. She was there; she saw the miracle firsthand; and she corrects them, describing what actually happened.

Since the rabbinic-era *beit midrash* was limited strictly to men, the image of a female biblical character entering and correcting the rabbis is quite dramatic. Perhaps this story—written by the rabbis themselves—gestures toward the fact that they, on some level, understood the limits of the male-dominated scholarly tradition. Perhaps, in creating a Serakh who can locate Joseph's bones when Moses cannot, the rabbis are subtly (unconsciously?) acknowledging that any tradition which does not fully include women's wisdom and lived experiences will have a compromised view of what it means to be human. It's not easy to acknowledge that our own experience is limited; I admire the rabbis for passing down a version of Serakh's story that implies the limits of their authority and knowledge.

Serakh is a quiet but powerful foremother. I love her radiant character, her multiple powers: her ability to use song as a healing medium, her confidence in the truth she has seen, and her mystically long—perhaps infinite—life.

Her abilities of perception, song, creativity, and communication are a beacon for the artist in each of us, the part of us that knows how to use our sensitivity to help others understand what we see. Serakh is a model for trusting our own experience; honoring the healing power of art and spiritual practice; and making beauty out of what we know to be true.

The Open Door Between Us

The beginning was coming to an end, the strange becoming familiar:

Rugelach from Marzipan Bakery, their chocolate almost burned, giving the edges a slight crispy shell, like a hint of crème brûlée lining the pastry.

The desert.

Shopping at the Machane Yehuda *shuk*, walking through the open-air market, the smell of butchered chickens that turned my stomach so I always walked quickly through the meat alley. The piles of sweets, the buckets of spices: turmeric, oregano, zaatar.

I washed my hands in the traditional way after waking up, before eating bread, after going to the bathroom, pouring up to my second knuckle from the two-handled cup: right hand, left hand, right hand, left hand.

On street signs and shop banners, the nonsensical squiggles arranged themselves firmly into Hebrew words. On the cucumber vendor's little chalkboard square in the *shuk*, *melafafonim*. On the central bus station, *Tachana Merkazit*. On the kiosk, *kiosk*.

Every couple of weeks, I walked to the Women's Section of the Western Wall and stood alone, surrounded by dozens of women I would never meet, each of us silently pressing her face to the cold stone.

At weddings, we celebrated until one a.m., even if the couple were strangers to us and we had been waved in while walking past a courtyard, because it was a mitzvah to gladden the bride and groom—men dancing with men, women dancing with women, scotch, sweet wine, treats soaked in honey and pistachios.

Light on olive trees.

Each morning, as soon as I woke up, I thanked God for returning my soul to me.

Evening prayers after sunset no matter where I was: An airport. A highway rest stop. Alone in my bedroom. Or in the safe walls of the yeshiva, which had come to feel like home, surrounded by the people who had come to be my closest friends.

The feeling of living in a video game where each street was seeded with points to be gathered and collected, scattered around the city, each mitzvah another hit of energy, each act of generosity releasing a spark back to the glowing, diffuse cloud of the Divine that I imagined hovering above us like a spaceship at all times.

I ate Shabbat dinner at the table of a family with eleven children dressed in matching clothes, whose parents opened their doors to travelers passing through, as they themselves had once been single travelers passing through this city, each having left their home to search for their ancient traditions.

I visited the turquoise-painted graves of Tzfat, the mystic city in the north where the great kabbalists are buried. Braided candles, light blue doorposts, the sunbaked studio of the artist who drew psychedelic Hebrew letters all day long. Wandering among the turquoise-painted tombs in a long skirt, I left a pebble on the grave of a rabbi, gone hundreds of years, whose poems I knew by heart.

The sanctification of daily life became natural. I learned which blessings to say when, marking time, history, seasons, the rhythms of my body: bowing and whispering until the words spilled from my tongue as if I had been saying them for all my life, or longer.

A scribe taught us to carve a goose feather with a sharp knife, to mix ink with a spoon, to write the *sofrut*—calligraphy, the way letters are written in a Torah scroll—on a piece of scraped leather parchment. Light glistened on the letters, tiny beads of ink that formed a necklace, long lines laid over and over and over themselves to tell the story of why I was here.

~

Many Friday nights during my first year in Jerusalem, Emily and I hosted Shabbat dinner. We cooked together all day, working around our tiny gas countertop stove, then hosted the meal itself on my bedroom floor. My possessions were spare, and transforming my bedroom into the dining room was simple. We flipped my twin mattress on its side, as we had on our first Shabbat. A few weeks into the year, we'd bought a large swath of velvet leopard-print material from the fabric vendor at the *shuk*, and we spread this on the tile floor to serve as a tablecloth, though we had no table.

The simplicity made it all the more beautiful. We sat cross-legged on the cold tile, a mess of hippie dresses and long hair, button-down white shirts, *peyes*, yarmulkes, sandals, laughing easily with each other. After kiddush, we'd line up in the kitchen to ritually wash hands with the two-handled pourer. We chanted the handwashing blessing, the challah blessing, the blessing after the meal. We discussed the week's Torah portion passionately, weaving together classic commentaries with our personal struggles, considering aloud how the ancient story might relate to our deepest feelings and challenges.

There was a custom of making a deflating sound—*psssssh*—to signify admiration if someone shared a particularly intense insight, or revealed something especially vulnerable.

I felt so close to Hashem today, as if I could feel His hand on my shoulder when I was praying. Psssshhhh.

The fire of the burning bush is the same fire that burns in front of the ark, the everlasting light, in every synagogue around the world. Psssshhhh.

∾

Here is what I still carry from that time: a mind full of Hebrew blessings; a bookshelf full of holy texts; the leopard-print velvet sheet, which my children help me tack on to the grape arbor every year to form the western wall of our sukkah.

∾

On this particular Shabbat, Emily and I had eight people coming over in an hour, more guests than usual; our tiny, sunny kitchen was at full capacity. We moved easily back and forth, sharing the two burners of our countertop stove, cutting cucumbers from the *shuk*, combining beans and ketchup and soy sauce and tomato sauce for the Saturday afternoon cholent that would cook overnight, baking tofu in the toaster oven, sautéing string beans.

In the midst of this chaos, a friend called to ask if she could bring someone to dinner; he'd arrive separately and might get there before her, but he needed a place to be. "Of course," I said as I dug a spatula beneath the baking tofu.

Our apartment was on the third floor of a typical West Jerusalem apartment building; a central stone staircase, open to the air, led to doors on each landing. When I heard the bell and opened the door, a stranger stood there: Nehemiah, late-afternoon daylight bright behind him. His eyes were too large. I could not look away from their blueness.

I thought *sky,* I thought *water,* I thought *robin's egg,* I thought *tchelet,* the color of the turquoise tiles that line God's heavenly throne.

We stood with the open door between us.

I could say recognition, I could say humor, I could say danger. I could say orchard, marble floor, waterfall, the green shoots of new plants. Sundials, planets, outer space.

Everything that would pass between us—the blossoming, and the falling, and me standing alone at his grave in the snow, halfway across the world—was contained in this moment.

But I didn't know it yet. Because we were, as we are always, at the beginning.

Part III

My Holy of Holies

Laughter echoed through our tiny living room as our friends streamed in, arriving from services at the various small synagogues nearby. All around us people were taking off their shoes, tossing jackets on the couch, bringing bottles of wine to the counter, chatting. Emily gave the garlicky string beans and tofu one last stir. Nehemiah and I did not speak, but we were exquisitely aware of each other—two animals in a clearing, watching each other in our peripheral vision.

Surrounded by the four walls of my sky-blue room, Shabbat dinner always felt to me a little like we were gathering in the heavens. Emily chanted kiddush over the wine, and as we all found our seats on the tile floor, Nehemiah and I found each other wordlessly, like magnets. We sat beside each other at the leopard-print tablecloth I had spread on the floor. We barely spoke to each other, but when our knees touched, neither of us moved.

The next day, I went to Shabbat lunch at the house of the friend who'd asked if I could host Nehemiah the night before. He was staying on her couch, since traveling on Shabbat was forbidden and his yeshiva was across town. My whole body buzzed when I saw him, and I thought I saw his cheeks flush when we sat across from each other. I watched him closely.

"Teach us a new song, Nehemiah," my friend said, and Nehemiah closed his eyes and took a deep breath. His voice filled the room with a melody he'd written. *Yah ribon olam,* he chanted, slowly. *V'almaya.* His voice was vulnerable, a little hoarse, like sun through a window. *He is magic,* I thought. Phrase by phrase, we joined our voices to his, and sang for a long time. Afterward, we sat in silence, the music still reverberating through our bodies.

And then, to my shock, he fell asleep at the table. I had seen old men drift off at a meal, but never someone my age. I felt a flutter of panic, of distance from my own longing.

Still, I vibrated all Shabbat with the jolt of meeting Nehemiah. I hummed his new melody as I helped with the dishes after lunch. On Sunday morning, I taught it to Emily on our walk to yeshiva. I thought about Nehemiah during every minute of morning classes, and at lunch, I was bringing my still-half-full plate to the kitchen when our mutual friend ran up to me, grinning. "Nehemiah asked for your number. Can I give it to him?"

He called that night. "Do you want to meet me for coffee sometime?" he asked, brave and sweet.

I thought of my vow not to pursue, or be pursued.

Then I thought of two birds following an internal, instinctual map, migrating to a sacred stone city for a meeting that would change their little bird-lives forever.

"Well," I said into the phone, "I should tell you, I decided I'm not going to date anyone this year. But it seems like I should make an exception for this. Do you know what I mean?"

"Yeah," he said, and I could hear him smiling. "I do."

Anton Chekhov: "My holy of holies is the human body."

The Israelite Women in Egypt

(Book of Exodus, Midrash)

Sex and love, partnership and power are woven through most human stories—and the Torah is no exception.

There's a repeated trope of biblical women using their sexuality in strategic ways to overcome obstacles and oppression. Ruth crawling into Boaz's tent, for example, or Tamar seducing her double-ex-father-in-law, Judah, or Judith, who dresses up during a time of war and sneaks into the tent of the enemy army's commander, Holofernes.

The Israelite women in Egypt use their sexuality, too—if not in the Torah, in rabbinic legend—but there is one key difference. Rather than seducing a wealthy landowner, powerful patriarch, or enemy general, these women face a different challenge. They need to convince their own husbands to sleep with them.

Their personal struggle has profound communal implications. Pharaoh is actively trying to destroy the Israelite community forever. One of his approaches is overwork: he drives the Israelite men so brutally that they have no energy left over for sex and are prevented from conceiving a next generation of Israelites.

So to continue their people, the Israelite women must entice their exhausted husbands, and they do so with a combination of sensuality, humor, and inventiveness. Their situation is dire, but their solution is lighthearted; according to the midrashic legend, they invite their husbands out into the orchard and tease them. The women hold up mirrors, saying, "Look, I'm more beautiful than you!"; they feed their husbands snacks of tiny fish; and during this desperate time, they find pleasure beneath fruit-bearing trees.

Stories of seduction usually focus on people who are not married to each other, and there is something surprising and delightful about a legend based on the difficulty of married people seducing their partners. Here, wives entice husbands, but we can transpose this story to any combination of genders. And no matter the gender, convincing a reluctant partner can pose challenges more intense and personal than seducing a stranger.

This midrash is focused on sexuality within lasting relationships, on intimacy that is not shiny and new, and the way it must be nurtured and tended to in order to stay strong. Maintaining love over decades, the story seems to suggest, requires play, humor, pleasure, and creativity. And, sometimes, work.

This story is linked to Passover, since it takes place in Pharaoh's Egypt, and it subtly connects to one of the holiday's most famous foods: charoset, a sweet mix of ingredients we eat at the seder each year.

Famously, tradition holds that charoset represents the mortar used by the enslaved Israelites in their forced labor—an element of the backbreaking work that was oppressing the husbands in our midrash. But it's so delicious, so full of abundance. And in another, lesser-known interpretation in the Talmud, Rabbi Levi suggests that we eat charoset on Passover to refer to the apple trees in this midrash, citing the Song of Songs as proof:

> *Who is this woman, arising from the desert, reclining upon her beloved?*
> *Under the apple tree I awakened you, it was there your mother conceived you.*

In my family, charoset is made by combining the intoxicating spice of cinnamon and the slight bitterness of walnuts with a bit of sweet wine. I think of that poignant mixture as I read this story about how we make a new generation together, the work and play of reproduction in all its forms. And the sacredness of this process is reflected in another legend: the very mirrors the women used to seduce their husbands would later be melted down to create the sacred washing-bowl of the Tabernacle.

Through the gentle labors of an entire generation of women, who tended the flame of sensuality, a new generation was born. Life and love continue, bravely and beautifully, in the face of all that would destroy them, all that would destroy us.

Upside-Down Coffee

On the way to Cafe Moda, it occurred to me that this was my first official date.

Up to this point, every single relationship had begun with a sort of sideways grasping, hands and mouths and limbs led together in a seemingly inexorable process too embarrassing to discuss in words, though apparently not to enact with our bodies.

Cafe Moda was Nehemiah's suggestion, which was good, because I would have been hard-pressed to name a place to meet outside the yeshiva. Occasionally I'd go see an art film at the Cinematheque just outside the gates of the old city, or busk on Ben Yehuda Street for extra cash, but otherwise I spent almost every waking hour in class, in shul, or at a holiday meal.

I took the number 18 bus up the hill to the city center. Nehemiah met me out front; we smiled shyly at each other and walked inside. I'd almost forgotten places like this existed, cute cafés with good music, like somewhere I would have hung out in New York—only kosher. Two women stood behind the counter, laughing loudly. When they saw Nehemiah, they turned toward him and called out his name in delight; I could tell he was not only a regular, but beloved. He introduced me to them as the owners.

They were in their late thirties, with long hair, loving eyes, and the gravelly voices of chain-smokers. They looked world-weary and wise; clearly they had been stunningly beautiful teenagers and had lived hard in the intervening decades. We took a seat at a corner table, and they returned to their gossiping, punctuated by occasional deep coughs. I could feel them watching us with auntie-like delight.

Nehemiah told me he came here as often as he could, though it was a half-hour bus ride from his yeshiva. Unlike my coed, progressive yeshiva, his was all men and strictly Orthodox. He loved the rigor and mysticism, but chafed against their politics and beliefs about gender.

One of the sisters walked over to us, winked, and asked what we wanted. I had no idea what to order at a café in Jerusalem; I followed Nehemiah's order of a *café hafuch kaful,* "double upside-down coffee."

Café hafuch turned out to be a work of art in coffee form. Part café au lait, part latte, part cappuccino, it came in a glass mug, and from the side you could see distinct stripes where the milk and coffee combined. Pure white foam on top, dark brown in the middle, a thick tan line below, then ochre at the bottom, darkening as the grounds slowly settled. Reminiscent of earth's geological strata, or a Rothko painting of the desert, this was the first of many double upside-down coffees with Nehemiah. Looking back, I can see that it was a kind of sacrament.

∾

Over our very first *café hafuch* together, we finally spoke for the first time, and it was easy. The whole café was lit with potential. Afterward, we walked side by side through the stone streets, pink in the setting sun. We were headed downhill, toward the neighborhood where I lived, and eventually we arrived at my door, still high on coffee and the overwhelming rush of energy between us, the tantalizing scent of marriage. We walked up the cool stairway and passed through the doorway where we had met, two weeks before. Alone in my room, we stood before each other in silence, savoring the distance between us, feeling the magnetic force pulling us together, and then he raised his hand to touch my jaw, and gently pulled my face toward his.

He had told me he was a wrestler in college, and I could feel his biceps beneath his button-down shirt, his hands large and gentle on the back of my head. He smelled faintly of cinnamon. We leaned our foreheads against each other, as if to meld into one. Our hands found each other, then our lips, and it felt less like a first kiss and more like a homecoming; our bodies so relieved to be together at last, we forgot everything else.

We followed each other down, both kneeling on my thin twin mattress on the floor, kissing each other hungrily, pulling each other in. And then we kept going. Fast, too fast, but neither of us could stop. I undid his belt on instinct, or by habit, or from desire. Still half-clothed, we kept our bodies apart while our hands worked beneath each other's clothes, thinking we'd stop but not stopping, until it was too late. Oops. We both looked down at his *tallit katan,* the sacred fringed garment men wear beneath their shirts. The pristine white fringes were sticky. Eros fell away suddenly, like a corn husk; we stood in the clear light of evening, horrified, barely able to look at each other.

In that moment, I am certain we were thinking the same thing. To kiss, to explore each other's bodies with reverence—fine. But we had met in a world where unmarried men and women did not touch. And we had gone beyond touching. What we had done was not dignified or sacred. We were drawn to each other with a force that was stronger than either of us could handle. It wasn't the sex itself but the loss of control that embarrassed us. We had meant to be intentional, to honor each step with the precision we had honed in yeshiva. Each time we ate, we said a blessing before lifting the food to our lips—but in this most sacred of moments, our bodies ran away from us, toward each other, to fulfill their animal needs.

In silence he stumbled across the room to get a Kleenex. Both our faces were red.

And yet we both knew that we would continue to meet at Cafe Moda, even if we would carefully avoid being alone together for a while.

~

The little round table in the corner of Cafe Moda was our table now. Nehemiah and I talked for hours, sipping the foam off our upside-down coffees. We talked and talked and talked in the tradition of Orthodox dating—any dating, really—that ritual trading of stories between the newly-in-love.

We told each other about our families, our respective ex-girlfriends and my ex-boyfriends, how we had come to this faraway place. He talked haltingly about his parents' divorce, how the fallout continued to reverberate, how much he loved his younger sister, how he worried about her. I told him what summers in Baltimore felt like, about *The Garden of Earthly Delights* on the dining room wall. He'd grown up with even less Judaism than I, but had been studying it longer. He told me his grandmother was a Radcliffe graduate, his parents hippie dropouts, that he was born on a natural-childbirth commune in Tennessee called The Farm. "I know about The Farm!" I told him. "The woman who ran its midwifery practice wrote *Spiritual Midwifery,* the book that inspired my mother to give birth to me at home."

We took this as a sign: The same wise midwife had inspired

both of our mothers during their births with us, on the other side of the world.

After a couple weeks, we went back to my apartment again, kissing carefully as if it were the first time—not just with each other, but with anyone. We began all over again. By this time, we were truly falling in love, and our physical relationship was easier to navigate. Being together felt sacred on every level, and for both of us, physical intimacy tied our earlier, nonreligious selves to our Jerusalem life together. Returning to our old standards of dating felt like an expression of the fact that our love was not merely circumstantial, not just a Jerusalem thing, but a true soul pairing, as if we could have met at any point in our lives and still fallen in love. It was part of showing up authentically, not to pretend to be more virgin than we were, to accept each other's sexuality as sacred. We trusted each other, had the same instinct: save sex for marriage, but everything else was kosher.

∾

Although Nehemiah was only a few years older than me, he quickly became my teacher. He was the only person I met in Jerusalem who talked about white privilege and racial injustice, at a time when it was less common for white people to bring this up. And he spoke, too, about the oppression of Palestinian people.

It is difficult to explain how much has changed since then, and how much remains the same. This was 1998, in a space between two intifadas—not a time of peace, but not a time of outright war, either. *Hamatzav,* the Israelis called it: the situation. A situation of flesh and blood, houses and land, bombs and gravestones, widows and grieving parents. In my American privilege, I felt neither safe nor unsafe. Some of my fellow students would not take the bus for fear of bombs, and the central train station was regularly shut down because of a backpack left on a bench, and armed guards were always eyeing my violin case suspiciously. But my time in Jerusalem fell between periods of active fighting.

The conflict felt foreign to me, as so much did here. I hadn't been raised to love Israel, or to hate it; I hadn't been raised to think about it at all. So much about this culture was inscrutable to me, with my American manners; I'd been raised to wait in line without shoving ahead, to respect personal space, not to yell at strangers or offer unsolicited advice on the street. As much as the *beit midrash* felt like home, on the streets of Jerusalem I felt like a tourist, a stranger. And that sense of being a stranger insulated me from a sense of responsibility for the suffering caused in the name of my religion, the suffering carried out in the name of the state that was founded to be a refuge for people like me.

And yet even then I knew that I was not entirely innocent. A rabbinical student doing her year of study at my yeshiva refused to attend Shabbat dinners across the green line that separated Israel from the settlements of the occupied West Bank, where some of our teachers lived; she said that doing so would support occupation of Palestinian lands, and I understood there was a prophetic justice in her actions. Nehemiah, too, held reverence for this holy land along with a deep shame for the suffering of non-Jewish people in a Jewish state. Along with the arcane prayers and the flowering of self-discovery I felt at finding my own people's ancient traditions, there was a hovering awareness that others had been forced out of their homes in order for me to be here. This awareness would trouble me more as the years went on, as I grew older, as I understood more.

In Baka, the neighborhood where I lived, most of the apartments looked much like ours—utilitarian, simple, modest, a small balcony the most exorbitant feature. But up the hill, there was a street of homes with a different spirit: ornate buildings with arched doorways, multiple stories, floors of painted tile in gorgeous reds, blues, yellows, browns. I marveled over the beauty of these homes for a few months before someone explained to me that they were the homes of Arab families who had left when the Israelis took over Jerusalem.

Left. An innocuous word for a family fleeing home. What does it take to leave a majestic house like that, where decades later I could still hear the echo of meals shared, dark-haired children running up the tiled stairs?

On the other hand, wasn't that what had happened in my childhood home, too, those suburban Maryland hills? The commercial four-lane Joppa Road, near my parents' house, had been a trading route created and maintained by Native people for centuries until it was "repurposed" by settlers in the late eighteenth century. That trading path became a defensive line to keep out the same people who had created it, until those people were driven away or killed. And fifty years before I was born, Joppa Road was paved over, to be traveled by the unfeeling tires of millions of cars. It is easy not to see ghosts, especially when they are not your own ancestors. I'd grown up going to Italian Gardens for family dinner in our station wagon, thinking only of the pizza we would eat as we drove down Joppa Road, and now I walked down Emek Refa'im to my yeshiva thinking only of the holy texts I would learn.

What is home, when the complex, cyclical mathematics of displacement and trauma seems to lie beneath every claim to land if you go far back enough? Someone flees persecution somewhere, and arrives elsewhere, only to displace those who were already there.

It is not easy to open our hearts to the ways in which we have played our part in a system of injustice—even if we never asked to play that role, never wanted it. Nehemiah helped me begin.

I mourn. I listen. I do my best to keep my eyes and heart open and to work toward justice as history unfolds.

∾

Nehemiah's strong hands always trembled a little, his eyes like semiprecious stones with a hint of fire. His knitted kippah—not the regular small kind most men wore, but a large rainbow cap that covered most of his head. His beautiful, heavy tallit, the prayer shawl he wore on Shabbat. When he held me in his gaze, my loneliness disappeared.

One day, he arrived at my apartment shaking. "The rabbis say so much racist and sexist shit every day at my yeshiva," he muttered. "I'm not sure how long I can last."

By the end of the year, I could read Hebrew more comfortably than Nehemiah could, although he'd been studying for longer. The language did not come easily to him. He struggled to translate the texts, yet he understood the ideas better than most of my teachers, as if he had always known the principles that lay beneath the words he could not decode.

His sapphire eyes, his wrestler's hands. I remember the feeling of slipping. *This is what they mean by falling in love,* I thought as I felt my feet lifted in the air, my whole body falling off the globe.

As I began to know Nehemiah's beauty more deeply, I also began to know his pain. "Can you lay your palm on my neck?" he would ask. The skin on the back of his neck was angry and red. I would hold my hand there as long as he wanted. He promised it helped, but eventually he'd shake it off and begin the involuntary movement that frightened me, drifting into a faraway look and making circles with his head, as if he were doing warm-ups in gym class. Slowly at first, the circles would gather speed until he was whipping his head like a tetherball. I remember my own embarrassment, then my shame at my embarrassment.

Protect ya neck, he would say, quoting Wu-Tang, and widen his eyes, smiling at me. His pain, he told me, was an energetic problem: a kundalini nonalignment. I didn't know what that meant, but I knew his suffering was profound. Dark and terrifying, just beneath the surface, linked to all the suffering in the world. I could sense it, but I could not understand it.

Engaged to Be Engaged

I was not the only one who came into the yeshiva early in the morning and left after dark; by that spring, a small group of us were so devoted to our studies that the yeshiva, previously a one-year experience, decided to create a program called Shana Bet—Year Two. Not only was Shana Bet free, it also came with a stipend for living expenses, and when Emily and I were accepted, we hugged each other and squealed, jumping up and down. Another year together!

But Nehemiah had to go back to America. He had run out of money, he told me, and couldn't physically handle another year in Jerusalem. The intensity was too much; he was so sensitive; his neck pain was getting worse. We were both relieved when he got a job for the next fall, working with Jewish college students on a Midwestern campus. We were confident that we could handle a year apart, knowing that after that, we'd be together for the rest of our lives.

~

That summer, Nehemiah visited me at my parents' house, where I'd returned for a few months before Shana Bet began. I was twenty-two years old, I'd gotten a summer job working on a boat in Baltimore Harbor, and I was so in love with Nehemiah that my calves ached. We talked openly about marriage, and my parents, who had gotten married at twenty-one themselves, trusted us. One night, as we all chatted in the kitchen, my mother disappeared upstairs, then came back down with Grandma Lee's diamond engagement ring. "You can use this," she said. That was how strong our love was, I thought: even my no-nonsense mother was swept up in it.

Before I returned to yeshiva, I drove seven hours north to Western Massachusetts to spend a couple weeks with Nehemiah in his homeland. Here, among the rivers and trees, I learned more about my love.

The Nehemiah I had known in Jerusalem was a glowing ember, a blue-eyed beacon, a mystical presence in a city that knew how to embrace a mystical presence. Here he went by his English name, Eric.

As he'd told me at Cafe Moda, Eric was born on The Farm, the homebirth commune run by a self-taught midwife with a master's degree in English. Some women went there to give birth, but Eric's parents had actually lived there when he was little; they were real hippies. They'd since divorced, so Eric drove me to meet both of them separately in the tiny, wooded town upriver where they each lived with their respective partners.

His mother's house was full of pictures of a guru she called Guru. Red-haired, very thin, and kind, she was Jewish by birth, but her spiritual practice was an Indian style of meditation, which she followed as strictly as a Hasid. If she missed her hour-long morning session, she did a double session in the afternoon. His father was a housepainter who lived in a large, rented house by the river with his much-younger girlfriend. She was about ten years older than me, had long chestnut hair, and seemed intelligent and sad.

When Nehemiah was Eric, and Eric was a teenager, his family (he told me) exploded spectacularly. From that moment onward, Eric considered himself the guardian of his lovely, vulnerable younger sister. We met her at a café later that week. She had tawny skin, lips the color of raspberries, limbs that might have been created by an ancient Greek sculptor. She had the sort of beauty that could turn a girl mean from power, but instead she seemed openhearted, trusting. I understood why Nehemiah saw himself as her protector.

I watched his mother watch Eric as he massaged his neck when he thought no one was looking. "Still hurting you?" she asked, concern in her voice. She turned to me and explained that Eric, always a good student, had to figure out how to pay for college. As captain of the high school wrestling team, he was accepted to Wesleyan on a full athletic scholarship. But during his first semester in college, a wrestling opponent threw him directly onto his head, snapping something in his neck. "I was there," his mother said, "I heard it pop." The injury was the end of his wrestling career and, his mother believed, the beginning of his chronic, unbearable pain.

Eric waved his hand away and smiled bashfully, dismissing this explanation. It was spiritual, he maintained, not physical; that's why doctors had never been able to help. He had already explained this to me: eventually he would heal himself with pot, prayer, and meditation, and until then, when the pain was too great, he tried to release it by swinging his head in circular motions.

During our two weeks together in Amherst, we practiced for the life we would soon live together. We walked in the woods, talked about Torah, slept in each other's arms, and went grocery shopping at the Stop & Shop. I could almost see the chunky legs of our future children in front of me in the flip-down seat as I pushed the rattly metal cart down the aisle, scanning packages for the tiny Orthodox Union symbol—a U with an O around it—that marked packaged food as kosher.

My stomach hurt constantly with the intensity of how much I loved him.

One day, pushing the grocery cart across the parking lot, we spoke of the future directly for the first time. We agreed that although we weren't quite ready to get married, we had both known since the moment we met at the doorway of my Jerusalem apartment that we were *bashert,* soulmates, destined for each other. "Let's be engaged to be engaged," he said, and I agreed, grinning wide.

Woman of Valor

(Book of Proverbs)

What is an ideal woman?

The ancient poem we call "A Woman of Valor"—in Hebrew, "Eshet Chayil"—asks this question, in its own declarative way. And people feel all sorts of ways about it.

Some read this poem (Proverbs 31) as a poetic expression of admiration for the Feminine: the worlds we weave, the magic we make. From this perspective, it's beautiful. In one tradition, these ancient words are chanted to one's wife, by candlelight, as the Sabbath begins. Everyone has gathered and is waiting to eat dinner, but first, we turn to honor the matriarch of the home.

Others point out that this depiction of the "ideal woman" (inherently sort of an offensive concept) involves said matriarch doing pretty much all the work, both inside and outside the home. Read this way, it's a troubling ode to the endless labor expected of women, who are assumed to have been the ones to cook the Sabbath meal, set the table, clean the house, get the children ready—then reap the benefits of a partner who sings a song extolling them for all their work, rather than actually sharing in the labor.

In addition to these two approaches, many other metaphorical interpretations of this poem exist across Jewish textual history. In these readings, the Woman of Valor is not a woman at all, but a concept.

In one interpretation, the entire poem is an allegorical love song to Torah itself. The great eleventh-century French rabbi Rashi states it simply: "Eshet Chayil? She is Torah." Hebrew is a gendered language, and "Torah" is a feminine word, which gives Rashi's assertion grammatic resonance.

Others interpret the Woman of Valor as an allegory for Wisdom. In Hebrew, Wisdom is "Chokhmah," a feminine word—and the book of Proverbs, where this poem lives, contains entire odes to Her. Wisdom, sometimes referred to as "Lady Wisdom," is addressed as a person rather than an idea. Proverbs 8, especially, closely echoes the language of Eshet Chayil. The former: "For Wisdom is better than rubies; no goods can equal her." The latter: "A woman of valor, who can find? Her worth is beyond that of rubies."

Taking a more mystical approach, others read Eshet Chayil as Shechinah, the feminine expression of God. In kabbalistic thought, the Shechinah is the Divine Presence, immanent rather than transcendent, similar to our contemporary understanding of Mother Earth: the embodied way in which God shows up in this world. In this kabbalistic understanding, the text of Eshet Chayil is actually a love song to God Herself.

I think this poem contains every single one of these stories. It is at once a list of oppressive and unrealistic labor expectations, a genuine expression of gratitude and awe for the incredible power and strength of women, and a metaphorical ode to Torah and Wisdom and the Feminine Divine Herself.

Perhaps one way to understand the heart of Eshet Chayil is as a series of questions. How can we rebalance our understanding of the Divine so that the Feminine is as present as the Masculine, both in our theology and in our relationship to our own inner divinity? How can we honor and respect the power and capability of the Feminine without asking Her—in each other, in ourselves—to shoulder every burden? How can we rise into interdependence, loving ourselves and each other, in our power and in our need? This poem's beauty lies not only in its imagery, but in the way it helps us name these powerful questions.

The Gates of Interpretation

My second year of yeshiva in Jerusalem was a heady, exhilarating blur of coffee and Torah. My first year, I'd stumbled through each line of the texts, looking up Hebrew and Aramaic roots in my clunky hardback dictionaries—Jastrow, Brown-Driver-Briggs, Strong's Concordance. Syllable by syllable I'd mapped the world like an ant crawling over a kitchen counter for the first time.

This year, instead of stumbling, I soared. I'd breached the barrier, cracked the code. The screen of translation removed, I could look directly into the teachings. They were blindingly bright. Each time I opened a book, a pipeline of energy dumped into me, a glittering transfusion.

The books filled my body with life force. I saw rainbow halos around the black letters. They vibrated on the page. *Black fire on white fire,* the rabbis said of Torah. At first, I thought this phrase was metaphor for the flame-like script of traditional calligraphy. Now I knew there was fire in the letters, fire in the teachings, fire in the repeated act of opening up a book and tasting thousands of years of experience, distilled.

As above, so below. The mystics say this earthly realm reflects another, more sacred world; the earthly Jerusalem is a rough translation of the sacred city above us. As a child, I stirred potions, whispering spells, trying to touch the mystery; as a teenager, I touched my tongue to a paper full of molecules, and saw beneath the visible world; now, I opened the Talmud and the letters swam, they rearranged themselves on the page, showing me hidden worlds.

~

Men and women were separated in prayer, unless the service was specifically designated as "egalitarian." It didn't feel good to be restricted from the men's side, where the Torah scroll and prayer leader were, but at the same time I loved to stand in the women's section, on our side of the *mechitza,* a divider made of wood or fabric—higher in stricter communities, lower in more modern ones. Even more, I loved the small, old, ultra-traditional synagogues in Jerusalem where the women's section was a tiny room on the second floor overlooking the main area, sometimes with a short curtain blocking the women from view. As a feminist, I knew that I should probably hate everything about that room. I wouldn't have wanted to live in that world, or pray there every week. But as a stranger, I found myself drawn to the privacy, the intensity, the anonymity of those small hidden spaces.

I liked separating out the zinging energy of sex and marriage in sacred space. I knew that the gender binary around which the tradition was structured was a gross oversimplification; I knew the deeply masculine parts of my being, and my love for women as well as men; I knew that in one way it made no sense at all to draw a line down the middle of a room and put men on one side and women on the other. And at the same time, in a space of all women, even old women I'd never say a word to, I felt a reverberation of frequencies.

At yeshiva, genders were separated in prayer but not study. I observed my women teachers, each brilliant in her field—Torah scholars, Talmud scholars, legal scholars, commentators, theologians. Most had three, four, five children. Every one of them knew that Rabbi Eliezer ben Hyrcanus, two thousand years ago, said: *May the words of the Torah be burned rather than entrusted to women.* My teachers also knew that a thousand years later, Maimonides allowed women's Torah study, though he did not encourage it: *Most women are not intellectually capable of study, but render words of Torah nonsense because of their ignorance.*

Looking for sexism in the ancient texts was like looking for racism in American history, like looking for oppression in the creation of a new nation-state where others had lived for centuries: it was inseparable, woven into the very fabric.

But my teachers knew the exceptions to the historic sexism, too, and could recite them by heart: passages about brilliant second-century female scholar Beruria, whom the Talmud says memorized three hundred laws in a single day; the eighteenth-century Hasidic community where a man was expected to teach his daughters Torah, though not Talmud or mysticism; the opinions of those Modern Orthodox rabbis and scholars who believed that women should have equal access to Talmud as well.

One of my favorite teachers was a mother of four who, as Orthodox halacha demanded of married women, covered her hair—in her case, wearing a different beret each day. During a lecture, she said: "I believe women and men are fundamentally different in some essential way. But if you try to tell me how, I will argue with every single thing you say."

According to legend, when the Israelites left Egypt, the Red Sea was supposed to split, but it stayed solid, as if waiting for someone to take the first step into the water. But no one dared; the people stood on the shore, doubting, afraid, the Egyptian army clamoring behind them, drawing closer. Finally, Nachshon ben Aminadav put his toe into the water. Only then did the seas part, and Moses and the people could cross safely to the other side.

Following Nachshon ben Aminadav's lead, one woman teacher in our community received independent ordination as an Orthodox rabbi. She was among the first in the world. My other women teachers simply called themselves "teachers," pushing women's leadership forward bit by bit while living fully inside Orthodox practice. Each decision had to be carefully weighed, balancing intellect and faith, devotion and critical thinking; they pored over rabbinic minority opinions, published books, argued their points.

I watched their courageous practice, which to me felt paradoxical, noble, and complex. Morning and night they studied these texts, devoting themselves fully—all the while knowing that many of the texts themselves, according to classic interpretations, dissuaded women from such devotion. Because my teachers also knew that while the Written Torah is immutable, the Oral Torah—the laws we observe, the interface of lived experience with rules, the beating heart of daily practice—is a living tradition, ever changing. As one of them liked to say, when faced with a sexist passage: *The gates of interpretation are always open.*

I had come to the gates of interpretation to find God, to find my traditions, and I had found them. But as I watched my Orthodox teachers cite proof texts for their right to observe the mitzvah of wearing a prayer shawl, I was beginning to feel a tug back to the world I had come from. The more I learned, the more I wondered what it would feel like to consider these traditions not as mandatory rules, but as helpful suggestions—to gather the glowing bits of wisdom to my heart, and let the rest sink back into the books.

I could still so easily remember what it felt like not to speak this language.

~

There were a few men who were neither teachers nor students at our yeshiva, but still spent their days studying Torah in the *beit midrash*. They seemed to me like lost sheep, sheltering in our school.

One such man seemed to take an interest in my studies. He was kind, shy, and unkempt, in ultra-Orthodox dress, with dandruff on his shoulders and a faint odor that floated from beneath his suit. We didn't speak to each other, but sometimes I felt him listening closely when I raised my hand to speak in the discussions after lectures. Once in a while he would raise his eyebrows and nod slowly after I made my point.

One day, he was waiting by the door as I left class. He motioned for me to follow him around the corner into an empty classroom. I followed without hesitation, knowing he would leave the door open, since ultra-Orthodox men would not be in a room alone with a woman. I was glad for this rule as I stood before him, surrounded by empty desks.

He took a deep breath and began, choosing his words carefully. "I've been watching you, and you have a special mind for Torah. This doesn't happen so often. You have a calling, an obligation. You need to use your mind for Torah."

"Okay," I said, "thank you, I'll try." Why did I suddenly feel unsafe?

"No, I mean it," he said. "You say okay, you say you'll try, but I've seen women like you, their minds are on fire for Torah, but then they get married and have five kids and drop off the face of the earth. You have to stick with it."

"That won't happen," I said. "Really. I'm not like that."

I turned to leave, but he held his hand up. "Stop, wait, I have something for you."

He rummaged in his briefcase, brow furrowed. Then his face brightened and he straightened, holding a thick double CD-ROM case. He held out the case to me, and I read: *The Bar-Ilan Four Part Digital Torah, All Classic Jewish Texts from Torah through Talmud, on Four CD-ROMs.*

I didn't want to take it. But maybe I was being unfair to this man; maybe I was gun-shy because of Chayim, whom I still dreaded I'd catch peering around a corner. I didn't want to make the same mistake twice, didn't want to give some secret signal that I was willing prey. I made a split-second decision to put up a wall. "Thank you, but I can't accept this," I said, trembling.

His face fell, his shoulders drooped. "But . . . why not?"

He looked so disappointed. The yeshiva was quiet, I heard the sound of a student laughing in the room next door. *He just wants to give me his blessing,* I thought. *The least I can do is to accept it.* I held out my hands and nodded. "Okay. Thank you." He placed the plastic square on my palms, careful not to touch me.

He nodded briskly and turned to leave. Then he shook his head, looked back at me, and narrowed his eyes for a moment. "The way you act . . . I mean, it's not like I'm giving you lingerie."

His eyes were unreadable as he said this. Then he left.

Lingerie. Here, where a man would leave an elevator rather than stand alone with a woman for the fifteen seconds between floors; where men and women nod to each other rather than shaking hands; the word reverberated in the room. I avoided him for the rest of the year, and I had the sense he was avoiding me too. I felt sorry for him. He seemed so lonely.

Two Flames Held Together

I was soaring now, my beginner days behind me. I was part of this community, part of this tradition. Like many of my friends here, I sometimes felt a tug back to the way I'd been raised, a little voice calling me home. I knew one day I'd have to listen to that voice, but not now. I had finally found a place where I made sense.

In late fall, a group of college students visited my yeshiva for a week, and we second-year students were asked to teach them a one-hour session. We could choose our own topic, and I decided to share my favorite teaching by a famously stormy, passionate Hasidic master. In the eighteenth century, Rebbe Nachman wrote about the danger of judging ourselves too harshly, the difficulty of loving ourselves. He urged us to find the points of goodness inside of each person, starting with others—which was easier—and finally working toward oneself. Each point of goodness, he wrote, was like a musical note, and in connecting them, we could discover the song of our own souls. *This is going to blow their minds,* I thought.

Not so long ago, I'd been in college, but the past eighteen months had taken me far from the young woman I was. Now I could talk about angels, the World to Come, fallen vessels, how long to wait between meat and milk. I knew the confessional prayers that we recited on Monday and Thursday mornings, the traveler's prayer we recited when leaving the city limits. I knew that loving-kindness was the fourth Divine attribute, aligned with the right side of the body and the first week of the omer, the seven weeks we count between Passover and Shavuot, a holiday I had not yet heard of when I was in college. I could not wait to teach. Perhaps I would grow into one of those women with five children and a classroom full of devoted students. I thought briefly of my promise to the man who had given me the CD-ROM.

I passed out Rebbe Nachman's teaching and we went around the room, the students reading out loud in English. Within minutes, I realized I had no idea what I was doing. Stripped of context, I could feel the words' heavy dullness. The students' voices grew more confused and bored with each paragraph. I suddenly remembered how, for years, my mind had glazed over at the mention of God.

I'd thought that being a good student would make me a good teacher, but I was wrong; this was going off the rails. We finally finished the page of text and I tried desperately to provoke the discussion I had expected to follow naturally, a conversation about loving ourselves, finding the beauty in our difficult emotions. My earnest questions were followed by silence. At the end of class, I handed out the blank evaluations I'd been given and returned to the *beit midrash,* embarrassed. I hid behind a giant book about the prohibition against gossiping.

The next day, alone in the yeshiva office to fill out some paperwork, I saw a folder labeled *Class Evaluations.* I couldn't help myself; I opened the folder. The first few were from the class taught by my study partner, a whip-smart guy brimming with charisma.

"Brilliant, so inspiring!" "Made me want to come study here when I graduate!" My heart beating loud in my ears, I shuffled through the papers until I saw my name. "I didn't get much out of this." "Not sure I understood what she was trying to say." "Honestly sort of boring."

My cheeks flushed as I closed the folder. Shame flooded my chest.

Later I would learn that teaching is like almost everything else: it can come as a gift, as it did to my study partner, but it can also be learned. And later I would learn to teach. But I was not ready yet. I was still just a student—though I was starting to feel a little old for that role as I stood there in the yeshiva's office, radiating with embarrassment at having snooped on my own failure.

~

In the middle of all this—long days studying, and long calls with Nehemiah most nights, the handset burning against my cheek, my phone card balance clicking lower—something surprising happened.

I fell in love with my classmate, just a little bit.

Hadar was different from the rest of us. She was a part-time student, daughter of a French mother and an American father, born and raised in Jerusalem. She had grown up secular, but was not on a grand spiritual quest; she came only to Advanced Talmud class, as if this were college instead of yeshiva. We wore long skirts; she wore jeans. Her fashion was casually chic, her English perfect.

There was something sad about Hadar that captivated me, the sense of a backstory I could never get her to tell me. She was beautiful, but not in a fussy way. She walked with the slight swagger of a high school basketball player. Her straight black hair hung down to her shoulders, and when she leaned over a book of Talmud, one shiny strand kept falling forward, no matter how many times she tucked it back behind her ear.

In Advanced Talmud class, Hadar and I were *chavrutas.* Half the time she didn't show up, but when she did, our learning sessions were fiery and precise. I had come to accept rabbinic logic, but she was relentless, probing into any assumption. *Why is it so wrong to be unmarried? What's so great about learning Torah, that someone should devote their entire life to it? How does that help the rest of the world?*

Why did it hurt me so much to hear those questions? What was I defending?

Meanwhile, back in America, Nehemiah had begun his job at the Midwestern college, then lost it almost immediately. He didn't want to talk about what had happened. He said he just needed to cut ties and move on, back to Amherst, where he found a job as a paraprofessional for special needs students at his old high school. We needed each other, we longed for each other. "Everything will be better when you're back," he said, and I agreed. We wrote epic emails, stayed up late on the phone; we pledged ourselves to each other over and over. We skirted around troublesome topics, anything tender or difficult. We just had to get through this year apart.

Consumed as I was with our passionate long-distance love, it didn't seem possible that I could yet again have one of those tantalizing, excruciating crushes that twisted me inside out.

But there I was, feeling that inexplicable, helpless tug to Hadar. My body would edge closer to hers without my permission, my nerves beginning to vibrate as our meeting time approached. She never told me in advance she wasn't coming to class, or explained why she missed it so often. Each time I realized she wasn't showing up, I felt a little tweak of despair.

The power this crush held over me made no sense, and I berated myself. As far as I knew, she was straight, for God's sake, and I had my faraway beloved. This gut-crushing longing had no point. Yet I was helpless to stop it. *Shomer negiya* couldn't help me, either; there was no social decorum around our friendship, no enforced distance, since I wasn't even supposed to consider feeling this way about another girl.

Had I learned nothing in eighteen months of spiritual study? Was I really back to the same hamster wheel of desire, obsessing over each time our hands brushed against each other, counting the hours until we met again?

~

For the spring holiday of Purim, Ashkenazi Jews eat hamantaschen, triangular cookies with jam or chocolate or prunes or poppy seeds in the center. These cookies symbolize the hat of evil Haman, who wished to kill the Jews in ancient Persia; as usual, we transmute the wish to destroy us into a tasty snack. Emily and I had baked them together the year before, filling our apartment with the sweet smell of dough, feeling the tiny crunch of seeds between our teeth.

We were at home, eating tofu and spinach for dinner, when I asked whether she wanted to host a hamantaschen-making party, or just bake them together like we did last year.

Something passed over Emily's face. She looked down, then told me that this year she'd be preparing for the holiday with my *chavruta*—the whip-smart guy, brimming with charisma, who'd received raves on the student evaluations of his class. Over the past few weeks, they'd discovered a mutual crush. The fact that they were making hamantaschen together, I knew, meant they were considering getting married. "Oh my gosh, Emily, how wonderful," I said, and I meant it.

After evening prayers, my roommate and my study partner walked together through the streets of Jerusalem, falling in love, while I returned to our apartment alone. They began to cohost dinners in his apartment. I knew they'd be married soon. And I knew I should feel nothing but joy for Emily—for my study partner too, but especially Emily, who had wanted this so badly since before we met. She had found the partner she deserved. It made so much sense. Even *I* could see it was a great love story.

But instead of joy for Emily, I felt heartbreak for myself. I could not let go of my own small loss, no matter how I tried. I hated myself as I cried in our empty apartment.

My own loneliness, that old familiar monster, was not gone. It had not been vanquished by the holy books, the halacha, the rituals. All along it had lurked just behind Emily's comforting, constant presence, behind the fiery hours I spent across the desk with my *chavruta,* in our own cocoon of intimacy. In their absence, I felt this loneliness coming for me, and its scent made me frantic.

I cried through morning prayers at yeshiva, drowning in loneliness and anger at myself. *All that spiritual practice for nothing,* I thought.

Meanwhile, my nighttime phone calls with Nehemiah grew difficult. Holding on to our love across the globe was exhausting. Pressing the hot phone to my ear, I heard a new desperation in his voice. On the long drive back from Ohio to Massachusetts, he left his wallet on a pay phone at a gas station, and when he realized, he pulled into a truck stop and called me at four in the morning Jerusalem time. He sounded frantic. "I need you here, Alicia."

The force that pulled me to Jerusalem had been vague, mystic, epic. Ancient hungers streaked through my veins. I'd had no idea what I would find. I had been open, so open. And now I felt with equal certainty that it was time to leave, even though there were two months left in the school year. I'd be breaking my fellowship agreement, deserting my study partners, and disappointing my teachers. It was embarrassing to leave like this, but I knew it in my heart: This chapter was over. Emily had found her *bashert;* now I needed to return to mine. I had been in school my whole life, and it was time to leave—to be an adult at last, to meet my destiny. "Remember the Stop & Shop parking lot where we promised to be engaged to be engaged?" he said over the phone. "It's time. Come home."

∾

He was right. I was from the diaspora and to the diaspora I would return, to the trees and smells and highways of my childhood. I would return to Nehemiah's side, to prepare for the moment when he would hold my grandmother's engagement ring out to me, an invitation to the future.

At twenty-three years old, I was a different person from the one who had left New York City two years ago. Grateful, brokenhearted, I packed seven boxes of books. I stuffed my big green backpack full of skirts and scarves, and bought a ticket home.

Emily never pointed out that I could have tried a little harder to be happy for her—not once. Instead, she hugged me shyly, looked over at me sadly as I stifled sobs during morning prayers. When I announced my departure, she insisted on hosting a goodbye party for me in our apartment, still decorated with the Hebrew words for the order of the seder we had painted on the wall last Passover. *Tzafun, Barech, Hallel, Nirtzah:* we find the hidden, we bless, we praise, the ceremony is complete.

So on my last Shabbat in Jerusalem, our yeshiva friends streamed into our apartment in their flowing dresses, their gold-threaded scarves.

It was the hour of *seudah shlishit,* the third meal, when the Sabbath begins to wane and the light turns bittersweet. We sang together until sunset and then, when we saw three stars in the sky above Jerusalem, we performed the Havdalah ritual, marking the end of Shabbat with a braided candle, its many wicks mixing into one large flame, and with sweet wine and spices.

With the Sabbath over, musical instruments were allowed again, and we pulled them out of their cases. Emily's guitar, my violin; more singing, more candles, more wine. I looked around at the friends who had gathered to celebrate me and say goodbye. How strange that I could feel so lonely and love these people so much.

We had invited Hadar, but I didn't expect her to come. These gatherings of starry-eyed newly religious Americans were not her scene; in fact, they seemed to repel her, with their devotional singing and Hebrew verses quoted in American accents, peppered with jokes about '80s TV shows.

Also, though I had a taste for dramatic goodbyes, Hadar struck me as one of those people who'd prefer to sneak out the back door.

But around nine p.m., the doorbell rang, and there she was, standing under the streetlight. "Oh my God, Hadar!" I hadn't expected to see her ever again; I was leaving in the morning, and I knew we wouldn't keep in touch, given how hard it was to pin her down when we lived in the same city.

Hadar came in, looking glamorous in her jeans. She said hello, sipped some whiskey, smiled politely for ten minutes, then tapped me on the shoulder. "Come on outside, I have something to give you."

We stepped out and closed the front door. It was a quiet night in the center of the Nachlaot neighborhood, moonlight shining cold on the narrow cobblestone streets. The old corrugated tin tacked to walls of the houses looked like a silver-and-brown quilt. I heard the voices from inside, the friends I was about to leave forever. I was going, not home exactly, but to a new place, a completely different life from the one I'd left. I was going to rejoin the man I loved, who was battling forces I could not see.

Hadar handed me a book, a modern novel in Hebrew. "This is one of my favorites," she said. "I wrote a note in the front. Read it after I leave. I really hope things go well for you back in the States, Alicia."

"Thanks, Hadar," I said. We stood for a moment in the quiet moonlight.

And then she leaned in for a kiss. A real kiss. A mouth-on-mouth, softness-of-two-women's-lips, three-dimensional kiss. It lasted four seconds, just long enough so there was no mistaking it for a normal goodbye kiss between friends. And then she turned and disappeared down Rechov Shabazi.

I never saw Hadar again, and I never read the book she gave me—my modern Hebrew was never good enough for a novel.

But I read her inscription: *At mevurechet u'mevarachet et kulam misvivech.* You are blessed and you bless those around you. I had never heard Hadar speak about blessings. I didn't know that language lived in her, secular skeptic that she was. But I needed this one, badly.

That kiss was one of the teachings I received in Jerusalem. All these years later, I am still unraveling the threads of what it meant:

That two people could love each other and not love each other at the same time; that even as I planned to marry a man two continents away, I could long for a woman who was sitting next to me; that in some way, she longed for me too. That the most important blessing could come not from my Torah teachers, not from a *chavruta,* but from a secular Israeli. Just a young woman, like me, looking for something.

Sometimes we encounter each other in a moment. Our souls join, like two flames held together, and when it is over, we separate just as easily.

If You Don't Take My Side, Who Will?

I had left Jerusalem in love with one person, and I arrived in Amherst to find another. Here, Nehemiah went by Eric. He was falling apart with such blinding speed that he convinced me that I was the one falling apart.

Eric's apartment in Amherst: thin beige carpet, fake-wood paneling, the sound of next door's tenants through the walls. We shared a gravel parking lot with them—three jovial stoner undergrads from UMass, with reggae stickers on their cars and recycling bins full of cheap beer cans. Just up the hill from our cramped, chilly apartment was the Dickinson Homestead, a stately yellow mansion where Emily Dickinson, alone in her little room, wrote about God and mystery. I'd shipped seven boxes of holy books back from Jerusalem, and I lined them up next to Eric's on the bookshelf.

We both agreed it would be better not to live together until we were married. But neither of us had money. We agreed I'd stay with him and split the rent until we both got on our feet.

∾

Eric kept the blinds drawn; the light bothered him. Synagogue felt like jail to him, so I went alone. He kept his weed and his bowls lined up on a shelf, and when I asked if he had always smoked this much, he snapped at me. "It's my medicine, I need it." And I realized this was true.

Eric loved the special needs students he worked with at the high school. He came home furious at the racial injustice of our system, how his class was almost entirely made up of Black and brown kids, and showed up each day eager to support them. But paperwork, meetings, and school politics were unbearable to him. "I don't know how long I'll last," he said. When I asked what he thought he might do instead, he bristled. "I need your unconditional love," he told me. "You're supposed to be on my side." And I realized this was true.

In the early hours of the day, when I woke up and nuzzled him, Eric held me in his broad arms and I remembered how it felt to simply love him, the way it felt in Jerusalem. "I wish you were always like this," he whispered to me one morning. "Once you wake up, you're so harsh." And I realized this was true.

I stepped into the refrigerator of this new life, the cold light of Eric's eyes, and the cozy certainties of the past two years faded. "Yeshiva is just a training ground for the spiritual challenges of real life," Eric said, and I blushed, thinking how pleased I had been at my own quick mind, as if quickness mattered. This was the true arena, where I was being tested, asked to see beyond myself.

Goodbye to the childish conviction that I was the star of a drama; hello to the dizzying revelation that I was just another bit player. I felt ashamed as I remembered crying at morning prayers at the yeshiva after Emily fell in love. Even in the holy city I was all about myself, grief-stricken to see my best friend's deepest wish come true. All that seeking just a smoke screen for ego, the monster inside me who cared only for myself.

These realizations lodged in my throat. It was hard to swallow, to breathe. But I was a good student, determined to learn to love Eric as he needed to be loved; to transcend my own needs to meet another's; to grow up at last.

Looking back, I want to say to myself, *You are enough. You don't have to save anyone. You can't.* But I wasn't ready for that lesson yet. *Tikkun,* I thought. *I have been training for this.*

~

The job posting on Craigslist flashed onscreen. *Part-time: Remedial Hebrew language teacher needed for small Jewish elementary school.*

I drove twenty minutes up Route 9, the winding road that connects the towns and villages of Western Massachusetts, and when I walked into the school building and saw the bright Hebrew letters taped to the hallway walls, some deep, weary part of me relaxed.

The school, founded by the local Jewish community five years before, was tiny but growing; begun with a handful of kindergarten students, it now went up to fourth grade. They rented space from a former Catholic school, a large, squat brick building with a few bright classrooms.

This is where I finally learned to teach.

Though my students were sweet kids—seven, eight, nine years old—they terrified me. I kept expecting them to stage a mutiny and expose the fact that I had no idea what I was doing. Every school day, I would wake at five thirty a.m., fear coursing through my body, and creep out of bed, trying not to wake Eric. I'd slip on my running shoes and jog through the woods of Amherst, going over lesson plans in my head as morning light filtered through the leaves, already turning brown in the early autumn.

But despite my anxiety, that elementary school was the one place I felt safe. It felt like a real-life diorama, this cheery, primary-color world, hallways covered in art projects, classrooms filled with loving adults and kids bursting with life. My "remedial Hebrew" class met in the stairwell, since all the classrooms were full. I looked up language-learning games on the internet, printed out Hebrew alphabet cards in the teachers' lounge. "When I hold up a letter," I said, "yell its name," and the stairwell echoed with children's voices: *"BET! RESH! SHIN!"*

Sometimes it felt like a one-room schoolhouse on the frontier, this tight-knit Jewish school in a distinctly Protestant corner of the world. With few teachers and limited space, everyone collaborated; the principal was a brilliant mentor, and I adored my colleagues, who took me beneath their wings as a brand-new teacher. I was five years younger than any of them, but we became friends. On Wednesdays, before teacher meetings, I smoked cigarettes behind the hedge with Idit, the rebellious, fifty-something Israeli Hebrew teacher, and Liz, the tender, butch first-grade teacher. On Friday afternoons, we held a mini-Shabbat service for the whole school; I played fiddle tunes, we sang traditional Friday night melodies, and then we all left for the weekend.

The kids loved my car, a twenty-year-old beat-up blue Buick my parents had handed down to me. I called the car Merkava, after the mystical chariot in Ezekiel's vision. Merkava was covered in spirals and stars from the week when a friend had borrowed it, then repaid me by decorating it with spray paint. On field trips, the kids loved to ride with me: the soft dark blue ceiling fabric had detached from the roof of the car and hung down like a tarp, and I let them tug on it from the back seat. "Just like the letters of Torah hang down instead of sitting on the lines like normal writing," I told them. The next day in class, I showed them what I had learned in *sofrut* class, how the scribe draws parallel lines on the parchment with a sharp knife, carves the feather, mixes the ink, then begins to write. Each letter begins at the top, just below the horizontal line, then journeys downward, the way the Torah comes to us from heaven.

∾

Each afternoon, I returned to the apartment I shared with Eric. I was saving up to move out, but one day Eric came home, looking downtrodden, and said, "They fired me."

Change felt impossible, the future frozen. In the month since I'd moved in, fall set in, and the space grew darker. The apartment had become a spiritual battleground, a pot-tinged cave of trials where I struggled against my ego as Eric wrestled with his demons.

How he suffered. He swung his head around on its axis, faster and faster like a moon orbiting. His neck throbbed red, he kneaded it constantly with his hand, begged me to rest my palm on it for half an hour at a time. I feared his mysterious pain, the power it held over both of us. "I need your compassion, Alicia, not your fear," he said. When I started to cry, he pulled me to him. "I'll figure it out," he said, kissing my head. "Don't worry, my love. I'll figure it all out."

Once, he whispered to me the visions he'd been hiding from doctors for years, knowing they would label them hallucinations—rabbis and demons battling in midair, blue light shooting through his spine. He never spoke about it again, and I never asked him.

The kabbalists believed we can choose between two ways of seeing the world: *mochin d'katnut,* the small mind, which cares only for ourselves, or *mochin d'gadlut,* the large, expansive mind, beyond ego. Buddhism had a similar concept, Eric told me, gesturing to the light blue book on his shelf by a Tibetan Buddhist teacher. "You are falling prey to small mind," he told me.

~

During this time, the simple rituals I'd learned held me. I lit candles, baked challah, whispered prayers. I put on my sneakers and jogged up the hill, past the house where Emily Dickinson wrote her poems, season after season, year after year. *Watch over me, Emily,* I prayed.

I wish I could say that I drew strength from the ancient stories I loved so much, but I was still too deep in my own story. They were there, though—these women, my mythic mothers—surrounding me, although I did not know it, forming a protective circle. Hagar, banished to the desert with her son, with no water in sight, who lifted her eyes and saw a well. Miriam, sent away by God for seven days, who returned to find that her people had refused to budge without her. Hannah, longing for what she saw every day but could not have, until she opened her heart, cried out, and rewrote her story. These women knew despair and loneliness. They also knew that despair and loneliness do not last forever.

A Self-Pollinating Tree

There is no darkness like the darkness of New England as fall turns into winter. Looking back, I have such compassion for both of us. We suffered wildly in that small, cold apartment. Eric, holding himself together by a thread, flailing to hold on to anything that could keep him afloat. And me, terrified of my own loneliness, utterly unable to hold on to myself in the face of his pain.

"You don't know what it's like to grow up poor," Eric said bitterly, and he was right. I was a child, I thought: a spoiled, overgrown twenty-three-year-old child.

My mother called to say hi. "Are you okay?" she asked. "You sound really sad." My kind mother, who would have done anything for me, who would have bought me a plane ticket back to Baltimore without a question. I swallowed and tried for a cheery voice. "No, Mom, I'm fine." It was time to grow up.

Sometimes I curled up in bed, crying, thinking. When I had finally cried myself into blankness, I thought, *Ah, finally, here it is:* mochin d'gadlut. *Transcend your small self, Alicia, and turn back to your* bashert.

For this, I'd decided, is what I had come here to learn: How to love. How to lose myself. How, at long last, to grow up. And Eric was a born teacher. He understood, like no one else I had ever met, that everything contains its opposite. As his pain took him over, I could still see inside him the sweet Nehemiah I had fallen in love with in Jerusalem: agile, humble, generous, kind.

But I also knew: I still lived in the world. And he lived in it less and less.

∾

Eric had a plan. His eyes shone; he had figured it out. He sat at the desktop computer, clicking, his face illuminated by the blue glow, while I studied the weekly Torah portion at the kitchen table, whispering the words to myself. I was far from Jerusalem, but the letters still shimmered and danced.

The plan, he explained, involved buying something on the internet—something about data—and distributing it so that other people could sell it, and he would get a percentage of each sale. He would no longer be poor. We would be set.

For three weeks, he stayed up late staring at the screen, picking at the keyboard, his eyes growing wider as he carried out his plan. One late fall night, the first snow falling in the Western Massachusetts darkness, the words I'd been trying to hold in flew out of my mouth. "That sounds like a pyramid scheme," I said, and Eric's face broke.

"That's not love," he said. "You're cutting me down when I need you the most."

I walked out into the snow alone to buy cigarettes at the Cumberland Farms convenience store down the hill—Eric called it Cumby's, local that he was, but I didn't want to be on informal terms with its fluorescent lights and the smell of purple cleaning liquid. I wanted to get cold enough to wish I were inside that apartment again. I wanted to see it all lit up, to see how cozy our lives looked from the outside.

By the time I returned from the store, I was freezing. I pulled my coat tight as I walked across the parking lot we shared with our neighbors. As my boots crunched on the gravel, I saw a glow coming from the window. When I opened the door I saw that Eric had covered the kitchen table with tea lights and lit every single one. Dozens and dozens of tiny flames.

It was beautiful.

I stomped the snow off my boots onto the mat. Without a word, he took me into his arms.

We held on tight to each other, my head bent onto his shoulder, his thick neck warm against my cheek. In that moment, two things happened. I remembered how much I loved Eric, and I knew that it was time to leave.

~

I had arrived only six months ago, but I felt years older.

The next morning, I lay in bed with Eric for a while, feeling the warmth of his strong arms, the worn white undershirt I knew so well, frayed around the neck. I got dressed, I made coffee. I sat at the kitchen table in the morning light and drank it. When Eric came into the kitchen, I told him.

He just nodded, as if he'd been waiting to hear these words. We went on a long, silent walk through the woods behind his house, and when we returned, I started packing my few possessions.

Tamar

(Book of Genesis)

Tamar crosses between worlds—from foreigner to tribeswoman, wife to widow. I wonder, *How did these journeys feel? Was she afraid? Was she lonely?*

Though we don't learn much about her origins, Tamar seems to join the Israelites through a series of tragic marriages within a single family. Her first husband dies by the hand of God, leaving her with no children. After his death, she marries his younger brother, so that he can care for her and provide her with a child; but he, too, is killed by God before that can happen. (Look up the word "onanism," if you aren't familiar, and you will know why Tamar does not get pregnant, as well as why God does away with her second husband, Onan.)

After Onan dies, Tamar is entitled to marry the third, youngest brother in the family. In fact his name is Shelah, which means "hers." But although Shelah *is* hers by law, Tamar's double-ex-father-in-law, Judah, is (understandably) afraid to lose a third son. He withholds Shelah from Tamar. This leaves her in a situation of extreme aloneness: no father, no husband, no children, no money, no land, no power, no family.

But just when it seems her story is over, Tamar rewrites it. If Judah will not give her his son, she will take what she needs from Judah himself.

It is sheep-shearing season. Tamar knows Judah will travel northward with his flocks. She covers herself with a veil, then waits at a crossroads called the Opening of the Eyes. Standing there, in the disguise of a sex worker, she invites Judah in. And he enters, with no idea who stands before him in the tent.

Judah wants to buy a night with Tamar but has no money, since he hasn't yet made it to the place where he will sell his wool. So Tamar makes him a deal. In exchange for the pleasure of her company, he will leave his signet and staff—a biblical-era ID. On his way back south, he'll stop by with the payment he owes her, and reclaim the objects he left as collateral.

But when he returns, she is nowhere to be found. Nothing for Judah to do but return home.

Tamar reappears in town months later, heavily pregnant, still unmarried. Judah, hearing the news, calls for her to be burned. But she calls him out in public, then displays his signet and staff, saying: *I am with child by the man to whom these belong.*

Finally, Judah recognizes Tamar. He *sees* her. He admits his fault in withholding Shelah, and the fact that he is the child's father; he remains by her side from this point on.

She turns out to be pregnant with twins, and the text is careful to tell us that from one of the twins will come the line of King David. This is also the line of the Messiah, a hint of an idea that one day in the distant future there will be no more hiddenness. All will be luminous, all revealed—and the seed will have been planted during Tamar's night of righteous deception in the tent.

But I am less interested in the shining future than the complicated present of the text. The nights and days of this strange pair, Tamar and Judah. His name means "gratitude"; she is named for the date palm, a tree that generally requires hand pollination—a form of reproduction involving human intervention.

I chew on the mysteries of the night they spent together, the flavor of my questions rich and earthy: How could Judah not recognize the woman whom he has twice married to his sons? Did he feel an eerie familiarity in the contours of her voice, the shape of her hands, her half-moon fingernails? And what went through Tamar's head as she pulled him close to her?

Judah seems not to see Tamar until it's almost too late—despite all their proximity, the crossed marriages, the obligations binding them together, the night spent together at the Opening of the Eyes.

Sometimes the one we love cannot truly see us, even if we see them every day. And sometimes *we* are the ones who cannot see what is happening inside those closest to us.

Judah the father-in-law, the grieving father, the businessman, the solo traveler, the one who fears losing what he has. Tamar the stranger, the wife, the widow, the veiled woman at the crossroads, the lover. The faces we present to each other; the mysteries inside us. The things we need; the ways we get them. How to be a desert; how to make rain.

The Buddhist teacher Sharon Salzberg tells the story of a dream she had once, deep inside a meditation retreat. A student asked her, "Why do we love people?" And inside her dream, she answered, "Because they see us."

A Place to Live

I held a permanent marker above a blank piece of paper and hesitated for a moment. Then I drew a house with a triangle roof, a chimney with smoke swirling up into the sky. It had a crossed square for a window and a rectangle for a door. *I NEED A PLACE TO LIVE,* I wrote, and below that: *Kind, respectful, 23-year-old teacher/fiddler seeks a household to join in Northampton!*

I cut the bottom of the page into tabs, wrote my name and phone number on each one, and drove across the river to Northampton. I'd decided that was where I wanted to live: it was larger, more cheerful, and ten minutes closer to the school where I taught. In mid-fall, Main Street was already glowing with holiday lights strung up high. They shone on the ice cream store and the record store and on my favorite café, Haymarket, which I loved for its hippie food and its queer, gorgeous counter staff. I clutched my hand-drawn flyer as I walked past Haymarket to the Masonic Street Laundromat. Thirty washers, thirty dryers, and my destination: a large bulletin board that served as a community announcement post for the whole town.

I walked up to the board and grabbed a pushpin. Then I stopped.

Before me on the bulletin board, right at my eye level, was a flyer with a house drawn on it in black Sharpie. It had a chimney with smoke curling upward in loose doodles. It had a rectangular door and a square window with crossed lines for panes. It was the twin to the house I'd drawn. Beneath it, in Sharpie, were the words COME LIVE WITH US!

The bottom had been cut into tabs with phone numbers for people to rip off. None were missing; someone must have just put this up, I thought. Heart racing, I tore the paper down, folded it up, put it in my pocket, and drove back to Amherst with a flying feeling, like I'd just kissed someone for the first time. I sat down at the kitchen table and picked up the phone.

I did not know, as I walked through the front door for the first time, that I would live in that house for the next four years, weaving a sort of family with my housemates, who were all twenty-somethings, like me. One was a massage therapist; the open pantry shelves were full of her herbs, drying in bunches and slowly steeping in tincture jars. Another was a sheep farmer, who told me how, each spring, he and his brother drank cream fresh from the cow mixed with maple syrup hot from the vat, so delicious they could not stop, so thick and rich they threw up afterward. The other two, a graphic designer and a high school teacher, lived downstairs.

They taught me about plants and stars, how to cross-country ski and drink scotch and bake sweet potatoes until they caramelized. On Friday nights, I cooked a big Shabbat meal; incredibly, it turned out that three of them were Jewish, although none of them were remotely observant, and the whole household began to join in, eating dinner in the candles' glow. Week by week, as we ate, laughed, and talked, we transformed from strangers to friends.

And finally the seasons settled into a calmer passage. My room was peaceful, with amber light in the afternoons, my violin case resting at the foot of my bed. I began to realize that the feeling of holiness I found in Jerusalem was here too—was everywhere, pulsing through everything. It just required a gentle alertness to notice it, like a radio tuned to the precise frequency, a clear signal.

∾

Trying yoga for the first time, on the top floor of a former Masonic temple on Main Street, I found myself in a sort of physical version of the *beit midrash.* It was a different medium of practice—the body instead of words—and yet I recognized the same rigor, focus, and peace, the same sense of transmission and training. In that bright, wide-open room, I felt the familiar stillness of the sacred. At the beginning of class, our teacher read from the Yoga Sutras: *In order to achieve a state of yoga, or union, one must develop both practice and detachment.* I thought of the *mishna* I had first read with Shira. *The work is not yours to complete, nor are you free to desist from it.*

In that open, light-filled space—sunny, with luscious, honey-colored wood floors—my body began to unfold, to teach me its language, to show itself to be full of the same chutes-and-ladders mysteries as the sacred texts.

For two years I had curled my spine over the sacred rectangles of Talmud and mysticism, learning the lessons of the soul. Now I unrolled my purple mat, creating a sacred rectangle on the floor: a space of practice, structure, rest, exploration. In this space, my bones and muscles began to unfurl, whispering their wisdom, which my teacher spoke aloud: Resting can be more advanced than striving. Caring for oneself can be a sign of wisdom rather than weakness. The body can store pain, but it can also help us release that pain.

During Savasana, lying flat on my back, I tried to let my bones and muscles relax completely, like a Shabbat of the body. I tried to let go.

~

In frozen winter, the sun set early. Fridays, in the wan afternoon hours, I prepared for Shabbat, filling our cozy house with the smells of baking challah and roast chicken and potatoes and wine.

As time went on, I met more Jewish people my age. A few went to synagogue; most were not observant. But together, we made a community. Most Friday nights, we gathered in my living room, where I led the evening prayers, as if we were in some Eastern European shtetl. Then my housemates joined; we brought steaming plates of chicken and challah and vegetables in from the kitchen and ate together in the warm glow, laughing.

Pine trees outside the window, weak sun sinking beneath the frozen horizon, chicken baking in the oven, covered with olive oil and paprika, table set for eight or ten or twelve. The ancient rituals of marking Jewish time, carried out in this small Western Massachusetts town.

~

I'd sometimes text Eric; sometimes he'd answer. Every six months or so, we'd meet for tea at the Haymarket Cafe. Each time I saw him, he smelled faintly of baby powder, as he always had, and my entire body remembered our love. But each time he also felt more distant, as if he were sinking slowly underwater. He'd spent time in the state hospital, he told me, and his eyes shone unbearably, like stars giving out their last radiance. There was a wildness to his old familiar neck movements, a desperation.

The last time I saw him, he glanced over his shoulder and nodded, even though no one was there, then smiled knowingly at me as if we had a secret. And then he apologized and rushed out the door.

~

Years later—after the cycles of time had picked me up, spun me, and put me down in a completely different place; after I'd moved across the country and become a mother of two young children—I got a message on my phone. It was from a yeshiva friend, the one who'd told me Nehemiah wanted my number, in Jerusalem so long ago.

I heard the news and thought of you. I am so sorry. He was such a sweet soul.

Eric Nehemiah was buried in a tiny Jewish cemetery in the Western Massachusetts woods he loved so much. The next winter, I went to visit his grave. It was a snowy day, the trees blanketed in white. I stood alone before his headstone and told him that I loved him. I placed a pebble on his grave, as is our tradition, and kissed the letters of his name.

I hope he felt me there, saying thank you, saying goodbye.

Part IV

Noah's Wife

Psychotherapist Esther Perel writes, of the problems she cannot solve for her patients: *I feel a small relief in knowing that sometimes there is no solution; there's just holding space for the hurt.*

The star of the Noah story, as told in the Torah, is of course the boatbuilder himself. Everyone else is a supporting actor. But none of us is a supporting actor in our own lives, and I wonder how Noah's wife would tell this story.

For starters, she'd have a name. The Torah doesn't give her one, though later tradition calls her Na'amah, or "pleasant," a name that feels almost cruel in the face of the Flood's suffering and destruction. Did she *feel* pleasant, or did she *act* pleasant but feel otherwise, or was she simply imagined that way by later generations?

There is very little in this story that would be pleasant for Noah's wife. First her husband hears the voice of God warning him about the Flood; either Noah's suffering from paranoia and delusions of grandeur, or he's truly hearing God's voice, in which case the entire planet is about to be destroyed.

Then she watches her husband build an enormous boat with his bare hands over the course of a week. Does she feel admiration at her husband's shipbuilding ability and his follow-through on a huge and complicated task? Or a growing desperation and resentment, as his focus is entirely consumed by this disturbing project?

Finally, they board the ark together and the rain begins to fall. There's no going back now, and I wonder: Was this the moment when she realized that only her immediate family and some animals would be saved, that she and Noah would be leaving the rest of the world behind to drown?

The list of the damned includes her parents, siblings, nephews, nieces; their friends, neighbors, and extended family; and every single person they've ever met. This terrible trauma—leaving everyone to their death and sailing away with her immediate family—is followed by forty days of unrelenting rain, flooding, and being cooped up with a bunch of animals (and their smells). Not to mention some very disturbing behavior by her husband and sons when the ark finally makes landfall.

Noah's wife is a cipher in this story. But reading it in the light of our own situation on our threatened planet, I wonder how our experience might relate. Are we, collectively, Noah—or are we Noah's wife?

I think of the great unknown we all face, and of Esther Perel's "small relief": *holding space for the hurt.*

Yes, we must act, like Noah and his family, to save our world: do what we can to prevent the flood, find ways to save those who are in danger of drowning. But there is also a tremendous human value in pausing to hold the pain inside us and around us.

The story of Noah—and his wife—is a heavy one, full of loss and destruction. But it ultimately ends on a note of hope as God hangs a rainbow in the sky. Promising that such destruction will never occur again; that there is a better way; that we can, and will, learn to care for one another and for the world.

The Mint Family

The human story, according to Genesis, begins in a garden. I thought of this often as my herbalist housemate taught me about plants, roots, seasons. In summer, we tinctured calendula petals, poured vodka over their bright orange and yellow exclamation points. We watched bees nuzzle into the open blue mouths of comfrey blossoms. We gathered the tiny scrolls of lavender flowers and dried them, and when the cold fall evenings came, we sprinkled them in hot baths, using this small pleasure to get us through the winter. We planted spring radishes, watching their red bulbs accrete just beneath the surface, and I wondered if watching this might have helped me understand, back in high school, that eating was a miracle and bodies were meant to blossom.

Hands in the dirt, I began to understand the earth-based elements of Jewish ritual more clearly. As the strawberry plants finished their cycle and the summer squash swelled, I began to see how much our traditions revolved around the stars, the moon, fruit, plants, soil. Three stars in the night sky signaled the end of one day and the beginning of the next, and the first sliver of the new moon marked the beginning of each month. In spring, we celebrated liberation with fresh parsley; in fall, we held palm fronds and myrtle and willow and the etrog fruit up to the sky, our hands full of the harvest, and shook them in six directions to express our gratitude; and near the winter solstice, we lit one more candle each night, calling on the sun to return.

The warm brown wood of my violin as I played alone in my room, how it had once been a tree. In fall, the New England forest aflame in shades of yellow and red. In winter, seven inches of snow. All my housemates had cross-country skis; they found an old pair in the basement for me, and we skied straight out our front door, up Main Street, and into the woods a mile away, joking and laughing as we went. Among the bare trees, we passed around a bar of chocolate and sipped whiskey from a flask, liquid burning our throats as the falling snowflakes pinged my red cheeks. It was my first time skiing, and I recited the prayer for new things, whispering the Hebrew words into the white blanket of sky: *Shehecheyanu, v'kiyimanu, v'higianu lazman hazeh.* Gratitude to One who created the world, for keeping me alive and bringing me to this precise moment.

∾

One day, out running errands in downtown Northampton, I passed a long-haired singer-songwriter busking on Main Street. To my surprise, I felt a sharp tug of envy as I dropped a dollar in his case, and I realized that although I loved playing music at the school, I missed playing out in the world.

A few days later, I carried my violin case a couple blocks to a spot across from the Haymarket Cafe and took a deep breath. Once I started, it was like I'd never stopped, and I slipped back into the comfortable rhythm of busking most days after school: playing tunes over and over in their jaunty cycles, slowing it down with the occasional waltz, people-watching as the music flowed out of me. When my wrists got sore from playing for too many hours in a row, I cooled them against a sweating pint glass of Guinness in the basement Irish bar down the block. Music and spiritual practice seemed to flow from the same source, ancient and transcendent. It didn't occur to me that soon I might have to choose between them.

One particularly beautiful fall day, I was sawing away in my usual spot when a tall, brown-haired guy walked by me with a guitar case. We gave each other the silent musicians' nod. An hour later, he appeared again, walking back from the other direction. This time he stopped in front of me, rested his case vertically on the ground, and leaned jauntily on it, listening as I played. One song, then two. After the third, he leaned over and dropped five dollars in my case. "Hey," he said, with another nod. "I'm Jase. I like your version of 'Skye Boat Song.'" I thanked him, we chatted, and within a few minutes we were playing tunes together, a crowd beginning to gather around us. It felt natural, as if we'd been doing it for years.

"I live just up the street," he said after a while. "Do you want to come have some tea and play some more?"

I thought for a moment. No weird vibes; he knew his old-time tunes. I was just a few blocks from my own house. "Sure, let me just pack up." I scooped the dollars out of my case and we were off.

I followed Jase up to his apartment, a second-floor walk-up above the local fancy-hippie restaurant. We chatted in the kitchen while he washed a bunch of grapes and set them out on a plate with some cheese. Then he left the room for a minute, and my eyes fell on an unopened envelope on the counter. I saw his last name and instantly understood that he was folk royalty.

I didn't mention the envelope when Jase came back, just took out my fiddle again and played music with him until my fingers were too tired to move. It took a couple more hangs for him to reveal his family status, and a few more for him to say, "I have these other two friends, a fiddler and a banjo player. The fiddler has an amazing voice, too, and they both write songs. Maybe the four of us should have a little session and see how it goes. Twin fiddles, guitar, banjo . . . sorta classic."

The next weekend, Jase drove me to the house where the fiddler and banjo player lived together in a cabin in the woods, half an hour away. Strong coffee with cream, homemade apple pie, small talk, and then when the conversation lulled we all looked at one another and shrugged—*Well, should we?*—and took out our instruments. The fiddler's voice was a rough and perfect alto with a warm vibrato and a world-weary edge, peaty scotch with a hint of R&B around the edges. I'd never heard anything like it. She and Jase had met as toddlers, they told me; she, too, had grown up in a touring folk-music family, and as little kids they'd both fallen asleep onstage at folk festivals, curled up beside the monitors as their parents sound-checked and the stars came out.

By the end of that night, it was clear: We had something real.

We set up a coffeehouse show the next month, and were invited back on the spot. Soon we were fielding invitations to play folk festivals and clubs for real money. The four of us made some sort of magic together: the guitar and banjo building structures for the double fiddles to soar over, the four-part harmony of our voices blending perfectly, finding one another's edges and pushing against them. The fact that half the band had famous last names didn't hurt, either. At our fourth show, in Woodstock, an older woman came up to me at the merch table. "I'm an intuit," she said, "but you don't have to be an intuit to know you guys are going to be big."

There was just one catch: Shabbat. For three years I'd held tightly to the laws, which prohibited instruments, electricity, money, and travel from Friday sundown to Saturday sundown. I had told Jase all about this when we first met, but he wasn't worried: "That's okay," he had said, "we'll work around it." And work around it we did, in increasingly Byzantine ways as we got more and more gigs. We scheduled shows that ended just minutes before sunset Friday, or found strangers' houses where I could stay within a few miles of a Saturday night show. The band would bring my gear to the venue and I'd walk over to meet them on Saturday afternoon, explaining to the sound person that I needed to wait until three stars appeared before I could join the sound check.

I was still teaching part-time, too. Between my job and Shabbat, the thought of touring as a band felt complicated to the point of impossibility, but we loved playing together, and this sort of connection didn't come along every day. We made it work, week after week: recorded a debut album, played more and more shows, pooled our earnings in the band account.

After a few months, Jase, the fiddler, and the banjo player all moved in together to a cozy stone house even deeper in the woods, two hours from my apartment. I stayed over after rehearsals; I had my own designated window seat there, a cozy space where I slept at night and curled up to read in the mornings. I treasured that little alcove, with its worn quilt and the trees just outside the window. In the morning, pancakes on the griddle, coffee steaming in the French press, we sat in our pajamas around the kitchen table and wrote new songs together. I kept one toothbrush at home, and one in their bathroom.

Another temporary home; another way station; another version of myself. I kept thinking maybe this was the last one, perhaps I'd finally arrived somewhere, and now things would stop changing.

To Build a Container

Performing came naturally for my bandmates, who'd grown up onstage. For me, it was a crucible. Playing on the street was easy; if people didn't like it, they could keep walking. But under the hot lights, an intense, cringing shame reverberated through my chest. Standing onstage, being *looked at,* expected to entertain, felt like a terrible dare. Still, it was a dare I could not resist. I was drawn to it again and again, sensing that there was a lesson here, something I needed to learn.

My yoga teacher had instructed us to observe our own emotions, like alligators swimming slowly in an aquarium. Ignoring them does not keep you safe, she said; naming them does. Only then can you can accept them; only then can you let them go. *I am feeling shame,* I thought, as I sang under the hot stage lights.

To cool the sensation, I closed my eyes and tried to submerge myself in the music, sinking deep beneath my thoughts into the simple pleasure of rhythm and melody. I imagined Grandma Syl smiling at me with the uncomplicated love of an ancestor. I tried to observe the shame as a tendency of my mind—the fear of being judged, or exiled, or alone. I chose to return, over and over, to the stage—a cave where I faced myself, lights in my eyes and nowhere to run, night after night.

I was getting old enough to notice patterns, how I seemed to find these places again and again. In the dark of Eric's apartment, in the loneliness of my last months in Jerusalem, in the now-distant reaches of childhood, I came up against the edges of myself, and wrestled all night, like Jacob, until I found the blessing hidden inside that vulnerability. As if only in that petal-soft, cringing place where my self touched the outside world could I learn who I was.

As if my pilgrimage to Jerusalem had been only one of many journeys, and somehow, after all those miles and hours, I was still at the beginning.

∾

Bands are like families, or lovers; each has its own system, language, way of being. This was my first real band, and as with first love, the highs were very high and the lows exceedingly low. I tried to stay out of my bandmates' dramatic backstage fights, and usually succeeded. We'd been together for a year, we'd met each other's siblings and parents and high school best friends, seen each other early in the morning and late at night. We still weren't famous, but as we catapulted quickly into regional success, it felt like maybe something truly great was about to happen. Being part of this group, this quartet, felt bigger than any one of us. I'd never wanted a career in classical music, and hadn't even considered that there were other ways to build a life in music; I'd been content to busk. As the four of us began to make a name as a band, ambition began to awaken in me.

Sometimes I had a sneaking sense that I was orbiting the three of them, now that they lived together two hours from me. I could feel that my Jewish practice and my dedication to the band were pulling me in different directions, that something had to give. But as we began to plan our second album together—the one that would really break through, that would make us household names in the folk world—I pushed those feelings down.

Not far from their house was a magical inn where we sometimes performed, run by a proprietor who was a patron of the arts, and who was happy to let us stay for free in the barn for a few nights. We planned a three-day retreat together there. We'd play from morning till night, working together to decide which songs from our live show would be on this new album, and rehearsing the arrangements.

For a while, I'd had a nagging feeling that a few of the original songs we played—indie-folk songs written by my bandmates—didn't fit well with the traditional material, the fiddle tunes and old folk songs that had drawn me in. But these songs were included on every version of the potential song list for the new album. It took until day three for me to gather my courage, clear my throat, and—as diplomatically as I could—wonder out loud if we definitely wanted to include those original songs.

A silent moment, and then some conversation back and forth—"So you don't like our songs?"—and for the rest of the day, the three of them looked at me in a way I recognized from Eric: *Why are you so critical?* They were unhappy with me, I could see that. But something in me felt proud, too, for speaking honestly. I had no idea that I was already teetering on the edge, and that this would push me over.

Back home after the retreat, I'd crashed hard into an afternoon nap, winter sunshine coming in my windows. My phone rang and woke me up, lit up with Jase's name. "Heyyyy, Jase!" I said, rubbing my eyes.

"Hi, Alicia," he answered. His tone was serious, and I sat up.

"Listen, Alicia, I've been talking with the rest of the band, and we just don't think this is working. I guess we have different opinions about the kind of band we want to be. And we thought that once you saw how good this was going to be, you'd reconsider Shabbat. So . . . we're going to continue as a trio from here on out. We'll play one more show together, and then we'll pay out what's yours in the band fund, and move on."

My stomach crumpled. Without them, I'd never be able to perform! Why had I opened my big mouth? "Please, Jase," I sobbed into the phone. "Give me another chance. I can be more flexible."

But his voice was cold, resolute, and I could imagine his unsmiling face on the other end of the line. "Sorry, Alicia, this is just what needs to happen."

For two days I cried, thinking about my toothbrush in their bathroom, the intricate arrangements we'd made, the pancakes and coffee and walks in the snow, and all the friends we'd made on the road—not individually, but as a band. I'd lost it all, I thought miserably. *What's wrong with me?*

And then I began to sense a spaciousness. Amidst the loss was also some possibility. No more fighting. No more leaving my house every weekend to live in someone else's house. No one telling me I was too harsh when I spoke up. It had taken me so long to learn the lesson of leaving Eric, and I was still learning it: even when I loved someone, I had to respect myself if I was going to survive.

Okay, I texted Jase. *You're right. It makes sense.*

The next week in yoga class, my teacher stopped at my mat. She squatted beside me casually and leaned her lithe fortysomething body in close, smiling, as if we had a secret. "I've been watching you," she said quietly. "You are very flexible, but you need to build a container."

The mystics teach that there is a fundamental balance between compassion and judgment in the universe, and in each of us. Between the energy of beginnings, and the energy of endings. Between love, and boundaries. Between freedom, and containers. To balance these energies within ourselves is an ongoing spiritual practice.

Being fired from a band, especially a band that feels like family, is humiliating. They sent out an email to our list letting everyone know that starting in two weeks they'd be a trio. Only one person wrote me back, saying: "God first. You always land on your feet." I played my last show with them at a famous folk club in Boston; after our last song, they did a press interview without me, hustling the journalist off to a booth as I stood alone with my violin case. For them, this was just the beginning; for me, it was the end.

As much as I loved the band, though, Jase was right: we weren't right for each other. And my yoga teacher was right, too: I needed to build a container for myself, to create a space for myself in the world. Not an ideal version of myself, not the person I wished I could be, or who my bandmates or lovers wanted me to be, or who the ancient traditions said a person should be. Just me, exactly as I was, flawed and human.

First, I just had to figure out who I was.

Vashti

(Book of Esther)

Esther is often seen as the center of the Purim story. But Vashti, her predecessor, is a fierce heroine in her own right. And in fact, it is Vashti's refusal to do as commanded—her boundary—that leaves the open space in the palace into which Esther steps.

It happens like this: Vashti's husband, King Ahasuerus, commands her to appear before a bunch of drunk men wearing her royal crown. Rather than compromise her dignity, she chooses to relinquish her role as queen, giving up the highest position in society.

In other words: Given the choice between power over others and power over her own life, Vashti chooses the latter.

But why does Vashti refuse to wear the crown for the king? As usual, there are multiple opinions in Jewish tradition. The most famous one suggests that the scroll leaves out one very important word: the king asked Vashti to appear before the people wearing *only* her royal crown.

Although it is not part of the original story, many Jewish commentators over the ages have integrated this into their understanding of the book of Esther, which makes sense; it goes a long way toward explaining Vashti's flat-out refusal to appear before the people.

Whether or not we accept the naked theory, the text is clear: Vashti refuses to comply with the king's desire that she display her beauty before hordes of drunk men. The king's advisers are horrified. They urge him to banish Vashti so that the women of the kingdom will not wonder if they, too, should begin to disobey their husbands. On their counsel, the king exiles Vashti from the palace.

It's not clear what exactly happens to Vashti after this. Some commentators imagine she is executed for good measure, others that she simply departs the palace. All we know for sure is that she leaves the job of queen vacant, to be filled by Esther, the conventional heroine of the Purim story. And here ends Vashti's tale, at least the part we know.

Among the rabbis of the ancient world, opinions on Vashti diverge. The Babylonian rabbis see this Persian queen as licentious and oversexed, an antisemitic tyrant—while the rabbis of ancient Palestine largely interpret her as wise and judicious.

Skip ahead fifteen hundred years, and the divide continues. Some modern interpreters portray Vashti as an imperious raven-haired villainess, the Evil Queen to Esther's Disney princess, while in feminist biblical scholarship, she becomes a heroine. In the nineteenth century, early Christian feminist Harriet Beecher Stowe describes Vashti's refusal as "the first stand for women's rights," and by the 1980s, Jewish feminists were celebrating her widely as well. Today, her story clearly resonates with the ongoing, growing awareness about how common it is for women to be sexually harassed.

But Vashti's situation also reflects another, even more fundamental question: What do we do when one thing is expected of us, but our instincts say to do something else? What happens when we refuse to dress up to appease the judgment of others, or even of ourselves? What happens when we see past what is expected of us and operate, instead, from what lives inside our hearts?

I wonder what lay ahead for Vashti. Perhaps she rejoiced in her independence and solitude, thrilled not to have to answer to anyone. Maybe she felt only relief and pity as she watched Esther assume the role she once held, and remained joyfully alone for the rest of her life.

Or maybe Vashti found some other beautiful, principled misfit to love, and they made a home together far from the palace of Shushan. Maybe, from a humble cottage, Vashti and her lover watched with pride as Esther, too, grew into her role as an activist queen.

Because that's what happens in the story: one queen's bravery follows another's, as Esther transforms from the voiceless girl who wins a beauty pageant into a woman who takes a great risk in revealing her own hidden identity.

Who knows, maybe Esther even snuck out once in a while to get advice from Vashti about how to handle the king. Maybe it was Vashti who counseled her to reveal who she really was—one queen teaching another how to be real, and in turn, how to save her people.

How to Make a Violin Cry

My second year of teaching at the elementary school, I was in charge of developing the Jewish Studies curriculum. I moved out of the stairwell and into my own classroom, where I scattered construction paper on the floor and called out the names of the colors in Hebrew while my fourth graders hopped like frogs from one to the other, laughing. I taught them the Mourner's Kaddish, knowing that they would need it one day, and as we practiced its solemn, incantatory rhythms together—*yishtabach, v'yitpa-ar, v'yitromam, v'yitnaseh*—I felt connected to every teacher who has ever stood in front of a room of children and felt knowledge pass through her body to the next generation.

After two years, I'd finally grown into my role as a teacher. But I was also learning to discern which containers fit me and which did not. I'd formed a bluegrass trio with two new friends, and the structure of an elementary school calendar was once again at odds with music. So when my students' parents began to ask if I'd be interested in work as a bar and bat mitzvah tutor, and the synagogue needed a leader for children's services, and a class for senior citizens at the JCC half an hour away called looking for a teacher, I said yes to all of them, and by the time the year was over, I'd cobbled together enough work to support myself. I gave notice at the school, and became a modern version of a wandering *melamed*—as my Eastern European ancestors would have called a Torah teacher who traveled from shtetl to shtetl, filling community needs as they arose.

I taught little kids whose parents wanted to pass on their Judaism but didn't feel comfortable in synagogue, and groups of retirees who wanted to learn about Torah without having to believe in God. I led learners' minyans in synagogue basements like the one I'd attended at Shira's synagogue, and organized the all-night Shavuot study session, and taught singing workshops about Hasidic *niggunim.* I filled the trunk of Merkava with holy books, and drove up and down I-91 throughout the seasons. Past the trees in their autumnal finery on October afternoons; gripping the wheel on icy roads on winter nights in January; drinking coffee from a travel mug on spring mornings, when forsythia bloomed beside the highway.

I recorded my students' Torah portions into my laptop, as my toupee-clad bat mitzvah tutor had once chanted mine onto cassette tape. I taught them the trope marks, which served as musical punctuation: the upward question of the *mercha,* semicolon of *etnachta,* the definitive ending of *sof pasuk.* In our lessons, we sat side by side like old-world *chavrutas,* and I asked them: *What do you love about your Torah portion, and what do you wonder about, and what do you disagree with?* We learned about the holidays and the women whose stories marked them, following the cycle of the seasons, focusing on each as it approached: Judith before Chanukah, Miriam before Passover, Esther and Vashti before Purim.

Meanwhile, I made friends with more musicians, sat in with more bands, traveled farther away for performances. Colleges began to book us, and some months I could almost pay rent just from music, especially in summer when the busking was good.

On one such summer day, after a lucrative busking session, I took the crumpled dollar bills out of my case and headed down to the record store to buy myself a present. In those CD days, browsing was still physical: flipping over white plastic cards with names on them, looking for a design or a title to call me, carrying the whole big rectangle to the counter, the clerk unlocking the clear plastic and sending me home with the square that contained the circle of music. In the world music bin, that day, I found an album called *Fidl.*

Not fiddle, but *fidl*—that distinctive Yiddish smashing-together of consonants, like potatoes in schmaltz. The fusion of those letters, rich with the fleshy, lip-smacking flavors of Ashkenazi Jewish culture: a warm oven, a cup of sweet wine.

At home, I unwrapped *Fidl* and slid it into the CD player. I'd heard klezmer melodies before, had even known how to play a few from the packet of sheet music Lenny gave me years ago on the street in Baltimore. But this was different, ethereal, mystical. The notes leaped upward, as if the bow were catching birds from the air, and the music cried and laughed at the same time—like a shofar that calls us to judgment, finds our lives broken, and loves us anyway.

And the artist—the great contemporary klezmer fiddler Alicia Svigals—shared my name. *How does she make her violin cry?* I wondered. Also, *Was there ever a* melamed *who was also a klezmer?* I couldn't be the first.

A few days later, over tea with a music-journalist friend, I tried to describe how much I loved the album. He nodded and smiled patiently as I went on and on. "Yeah," my friend said, "it's a killer album." He stirred his tea, licked the spoon, and shrugged. "Well, why don't you go take a lesson with her? She lives in New York. I can connect you two."

∾

Alicia's apartment was three hours' drive from Northampton, and only a few blocks from my college dorm room. I walked past the bagel-egg-and-cheese carts, the familiar hexagonal flagstones of Riverside Park. In the air-conditioned elevator, I held my violin case close. Alicia opened the door to her apartment and smiled warmly, her tight graying curls brushing her shoulders. Her apartment's entrance was hung with pictures of the family: Alicia and her wife, their son with his cello. It had been over a decade since I'd had a violin lesson that wasn't in a bar or on a street corner, and I felt awkward. I unzipped my case and took out my instrument.

"Flick your pinkie against the fingerboard," Alicia instructed me. "Now play a trill on a half step—roll your hand instead of moving the higher finger up and down." I heard a new sound resonating from my instrument: a high, reaching sob. Moving and startling, familiar and uncanny, like hearing my own voice speak in a different accent. "Try ending a note on an up-bow." She picked up her own violin and showed me how to make the bow so light on the strings that the sound called forth ghosts, opening a new path between my heart and my fingers, one that led backward in time, to the songs my own great-great-grandparents would have danced to at their weddings in the villages of Eastern Europe.

Six months later, an email arrived out of the blue. *My name is Annette, and I'm the bandleader of Golem, a klezmer rock band in New York City. We are looking for a violinist and you have been recommended to us. Would you like to audition?*

The Band Agrees

Annette played a small red accordion, studded with rhinestones, which she strapped to her chest; I tightened my blue carbon-fiber bow. She'd driven up from New York to audition me; I'd given her water and showed her the bathroom, we'd chatted awkwardly on the mustard-yellow couch in the living room, and then we finally got down to business, leaning over at the same time to unzip our cases and lift our instruments from the floor.

I'd looked up Golem online the minute I read Annette's email. They were an unlikely band, a once-in-a-lifetime, one-in-a-million, *bashert* crew of genius musical misfits who played klezmer with a wild punk rock aesthetic. Of course they were named after a legendary Jewish monster from Prague. In the video I watched, frighteningly talented musicians hopped around the stage: playing accordion, tambourines, horns, and drums, they were sweaty, possibly drunk, all dressed in red, playing their asses off.

I found out later that Annette had already scoured New York for available klezmer fiddlers and come up empty-handed. In desperation she'd asked Alicia, the master fiddler of the Upper West Side, for help. "Well," Alicia told her, "I have no idea what she's up to, but this young woman from Massachusetts who took a couple lessons with me last year seems like she might be a good match . . ."

I responded to Annette: *I love your band but I have to tell you up front, I don't play on Shabbat, and I totally understand if that doesn't work for you.*

I hesitated for a moment, then added, *ps: I'm open to maybe playing Saturdays, but not Friday night.* I took a deep breath and pressed send.

Let's just meet and see what happens, Annette had responded.

And now here we were, playing the songs we both knew at my audition in my own living room, filling the air with melodies from Eastern Europe—songs my grandmother learned from her mother, songs I'd learned from the manila envelope the harmonica player had handed me on the street in Baltimore years ago. I watched Annette out of the corner of my eye while we played. She wore high-heeled sandals, her toenails painted dark blue, her knee bobbing up and down to the beat, the black curls of her hair brushing her shoulders as she dragged the accordion bellows emphatically back and forth.

After an hour, we took a break for tea, and Annette followed me into our sunny kitchen. "Black, with two sugars please," she said. Physically tiny, she moved with the grace of a former ballerina but somehow projected the power of a lion. I thought I'd played well, but if she was impressed, she didn't show it.

But the next afternoon, Annette emailed, inviting me to audition formally in Brooklyn. This time, the whole band would be present. I drove the three hours south—Interstate 91 to the Triboro Bridge to the Brooklyn-Queens Expressway—to their drummer's apartment. Instruments leaning against walls, beer cans, white tile floor, amps plugged into the wall, old tapestries—it had the familiar dank smell of a basement practice space, and felt like home.

The band slowly assembled, and we shared a French press of coffee in mismatched mugs, some small talk about what everyone was listening to—then we picked up our instruments. Silence filled the damp basement. Annette cued me to improvise, nodding with her chin as her hands tugged the accordion, which moaned a D-minor chord. The drummer's eyes shone as he settled into the beat, the lanky redheaded bass player draped over his instrument, nodding encouragingly at me as I began to play. The trombonist and I harmonized together easily, smiling at each other, then looking away shyly as our melodies twined together.

We launched into a traditional song, and Annette traded verses with the other front person, who howled into the microphone in Yiddish while he slammed the tambourine into his thigh. He was clearly the jester of the band and kept a running monologue going between songs—jokes, impersonations, commentary, interspersed with friendly jabs at the other musicians. After a while, he tentatively began to direct some gentle jokes at me, watching closely to see if I could handle it. By the end of the two-hour practice, he teased me openly, as if we'd known each other for years. I loved it.

The next week, Annette called. "The band agrees," she said, "if you move to New York and join us, we'll stop playing on Friday nights. We never get our best crowds then anyway."

My breath caught in my throat. Professional musicians deciding not to play on Friday night? This was a declaration of love, outlandish, ridiculous. "Yes," I said. "Wow, amazing, thank you, yes!"

It was a dream I had not dared to admit even to myself, to have my Jewish self and my musician self merge. And so in 2004, I moved back to New York City to play fiddle in Golem, returning to my ancestral land of concrete, car alarms, cigarettes. I sublet a room in Brooklyn, one mile from where my Grandma Lee had grown up.

~

My urban shell regrew quickly. I relished the toughness of New York, the protection, the container. I found a part-time job as a deckhand on the water taxi, staring dreamily at the Manhattan and Brooklyn skylines as we motored back and forth across the East River, shouting *Please watch your step!* as tourists disembarked on each stop. Meanwhile, in rehearsal, I began to relax—I was getting to know the band better, slowly becoming part of their living organism. While I played, I studied Annette, who was a few years older than me, and unlike anyone I'd ever met—equally adept at learning languages (she spoke five) and dancing sensuously onstage.

Before my first official show with the band in Brooklyn, perched on a ratty couch backstage, trimming my nails so they wouldn't dig into the violin's fingerboard, I felt a rush of joy and turned to Annette. "Isn't this an amazing job," I said to her, "to get paid to make music with friends?"

She looked directly at me. "We're not friends," she said flatly, and then looked away.

It was true, we barely knew each other. Plus, as bandleader, she was my boss. I felt a little embarrassed, but also defiant. *We're going to be friends, dammit,* I thought. *Just you watch.*

When we toured, Annette and I shared a room; it only took a couple months before we knew each other's secrets. *Ha,* I thought. *I knew it.*

Besides her many languages, Annette was fluent in a dialect of a womanhood I'd never learned: how to dress, how to dance, how to use liquid eyeliner. My mom didn't know these things, and when I'd gone out in the world in my early twenties, I'd been too busy wrestling with ancient alphabets and taming my inner demons. Dressing up sexy, I'd always assumed, was out of reach for a dork like me. But Annette, musicologist and linguist that she was, didn't see a conflict between being a brainiac and being unapologetically hot.

I had assumed my thrown-together hybrid of punky-cute, hippie-careless, and thrift-store-weirdo would be my look for life. But as I entered my late twenties, I began to realize that, like so much else, hotness can be a learned behavior. In a sort of *chavruta*, I taught Annette the Hasidic wedding songs I'd learned in Jerusalem, and she taught me how to dress. She took me to buy my first bikini that actually fit, replacing my stretched-out old boy shorts. We scoured the cheap fashion stores on Union Square, where I bought my first tube dress—red on the top, black on the bottom.

After so many years of thrift-store flannels and hippie skirts, dressing up thrilled me. I traded my long skirts for miniskirts, overalls for skinny jeans. I wandered into a fancy boutique in Park Slope, which smelled of gardenia candles, where the shopkeeper found jeans that fit me perfectly, and encouraged me to divide their astronomical price by the number of days I would wear them. Golem's wedding gigs paid well enough that I had a little extra money for the first time; I bought the jeans.

As I'd once learned the words of the morning prayers, I now learned the intricacies of mascara and lipstick, blush and bronzer. I began to wear simple makeup for the first time, not just onstage, but on regular days. I made an appointment to have my hair highlighted for the first time at a hipster salon down the block from my apartment. It was decorated entirely with a mermaid theme and I figured it couldn't be too expensive, with such funky wall hangings. I was too shy to ask for the cost beforehand, and when it came time to pay, the woman casually said a number so high I couldn't breathe for a moment. I paid, then texted Annette in embarrassment. But she wrote back, "I'm proud of you! Your hair is an outfit you wear every day."

Sexual power in New York was an accepted form of currency, of communication. In college I'd been too young, too concerned with my books to notice. Now I saw it: a secret conversation that ran through the streets, the subway, the day, matter-of-fact, without shame or a second thought. I felt myself on the inside of it for the first time.

Growing up, I'd accepted what the Puritan-inflected society around me taught: sexuality and the sacred were two distinct channels, without any overlap. On one hand, sex and partying; on the other, modesty and devotion to the Divine.

But many traditions, including Judaism, also teach about the sacredness of sexuality. In yeshiva, I'd studied the ancient text requiring a man to satisfy his wife, prescribing—if and only if she wishes—that husbands show up for regular sex, with the required frequency based on their jobs. (Sailors less often than laborers, since their work takes them away from home.) Jewish mysticism, in particular, understands sexual energy to be a driving force of the universe, in which a transcendent God and an immanent God(dess) are in exile from each other six days a week, longing for each other until they unite in cosmic union on Shabbat.

Living in a body is messy, each era in its own specific way. I was beginning to grow into my own center of gravity, gathering substance at my core, a certain self-ness taking hold, the book of my life now partially written. I'd found a steady stream of bar and bat mitzvah students to tutor at the local synagogue in Brooklyn, which worked beautifully with our tour schedule. I was taking what I had learned and giving it back to the world.

The Ability to Return

In the green room, dressed in red and black, Annette and I looked upward to heaven as we applied mascara, rubbed blush onto the apples of our cheeks, leaned in toward the mirror as we painted on red lipstick. I joined the boys in ritual shots of scotch, slivovitz, vodka, waiting until it was time to go on. When the signal came, the six of us strutted out onto the stage, plugging in our instruments, squinting against the lights. We looked toward our drummer, waiting for him to play the run of sixteenth notes that led into the first wild, raucous bars, and then we all dove in, Annette tugging on her sparkly red accordion and wailing in Yiddish, *How dear you are to me, O city of Odessa!*

On the road, we were a family. I'd never felt safer than I felt hurtling down the New Jersey Turnpike in that van, with the drums and accordion all packed up in the back. Once, we stopped for gas on I-80 in Pennsylvania and I saw a swastika etched into the bathroom stall. Playing these songs night after night in Yiddish, the language of my ancestors, even if I couldn't speak it, felt like resistance, survival.

The trombonist stared at his laptop screen with headphones, remixing jazz songs beside me. Annette tapped furiously on her phone, confirming hotel and load-in time for the next night's show, while the other guys passed around a joint and tried to out-obscure each other with musical references. We argued, laughed, rehearsed, debated. Sometimes one of us would get too drunk to walk, and the rest of us would carry them to their hotel bed. The joy I'd felt with my Jerusalem friends as we surrendered ourselves entirely to Torah, letting it live in us, becoming vessels for its light—now I felt it again with another ancient guild I belonged to: musicians, wandering troubadours, entertainers, klezmorim.

My violin and my Jewishness were at last one, inseparable, as I pranced around onstage playing klezmer fiddle in a red-and-black minidress. The same tingly buzz of holiness I used to feel walking through the streets of Jerusalem covered in a flowing dress, I felt onstage with Golem late at night, stage lights on my bare arms, the mystery, the Divine, the essence of life itself coursing through our bodies as we played.

The exquisite shame of performance did not leave me, but with Annette by my side, and the rest of the band to my right and left, it lessened. Our tours were short, and we often performed in town, so it was easy to combine my music life with teaching Torah—to children and, increasingly, to adults as well. Time passed quickly, greased by my happiness.

The Feral Cat Guitar

In traditional Torah learning, historical facts are mostly extraneous. This form of study is rooted firmly in the realm of myth, of transtemporal truths. In this worldview, the Torah was given to Moses on Sinai; the mystical Zohar was found in a drawer in Spain a thousand years after it was written; Elijah the prophet and Serakh the singer both hover above us, immortal and benevolent, visiting occasionally. Whether or not these are literally "true" is immaterial; their poetic truth is enough.

But as my adult students pushed me further, asking questions about facts and history, I realized that I also wanted to understand more about historical scholarship. And if I was going to support myself as an artist, and support a family one day, maybe it was time to think about going back to school.

Rabbinical school was the obvious answer. I was still more observant than anyone had been in three generations of my family, more observant than anyone I'd met until I was eighteen years old. I thought of the rabbi's aside at my bat mitzvah—*She should be a rabbi!*—and the profound peace that filled me when I saw a page of Talmud, its patchwork quilt of Hebrew letters, a collaborative performance project searching for God in the nooks and crannies of everyday life. I loved teaching Torah, loved to hold the match of my own seeking to the kindling of another person's seeking. Sometimes, sitting with a student, I felt the rabbis' teachings shoot through me like fire; I was just a vessel, an opening from the ancient wisdom to my students who sat beside me. And then there was the matter of my last name, or what it would have been if my grandfather hadn't changed it: Rabinowitz, son of a rabbi. *Rabbi Rabins.*

But then what would happen to the other Alicia, the one in the short red-and-black dress, sitting in a pot-filled green room, laughing, clutching her violin and bow with one hand, feeling that this, too, was home? How could I speak my mind as a rabbi without claiming to represent my entire community, which I had no desire to do? How could I continue to drop f-bombs with abandon? What container could hold me?

The application deadline fast approaching, I found myself unable to decide. So when a musician friend called to say he had free tickets to a Wilco concert, I jumped at the chance to escape my own brain. We rode the subway together to a huge, fancy theater in Midtown, and climbed up two flights of carpeted stairs to find our seats in the balcony, where my fear of heights made every breath both thrilling and nauseating.

Perched on our red velvet cushions, waiting for the band to come onstage, my friend and I filled each other in on what was happening in our lives. He'd begun touring with one of his bluegrass idols; his career was finally taking off. For my part, I was frozen between two paths. Desperate, I asked what he thought. He was silent for a moment, then he looked at me. "Well, I can't answer it for you, but I will say there's an energy that comes off you when you're making music, or writing, or whatever," he said slowly. "And it just seems sort of . . . you."

The band walked onstage, tiny figures picking up their guitars far below, and as they strapped their instruments over their shoulders I knew he was right. Rabbi was not the right container, not now. I applied to graduate school instead.

For the next two years, I took the subway from Brooklyn to the Upper West Side three days a week. I climbed up the stairs of the 116th Street entrance, my home stop during my four years of college, and took my seat in campus classrooms, like an older echo of my past self. But I was a different person now, with different questions. What did our tradition say about women who played music? I knew there were fraught questions about women singing within Orthodoxy because of modesty concerns, but what about our ancient and medieval legends? Could I connect to a sisterhood of Jewish women musicians across time, even if my sisters were mythical, even if I had to connect to them through the words of men?

I dove into research. Some legends portrayed women musicians as leaders to be emulated. Others described them as dangerous, incendiary, destructive. *Either way,* I thought, *they are saying we are powerful.*

And beneath the question of music in these women's lives was another question: of what it meant to be human, and a woman, across generations. Of how they might have experienced their own emotional struggles, and how they might keep me company in my own. A decade since I'd first encountered these biblical stories in Jerusalem, I was ready to understand them in a new way. Miriam, who led the Israelites since girlhood but was exiled for a week for questioning her younger brother Moses; the general and prophetess Deborah, who sang beneath a palm tree; Rachel and Leah's story of sisterly rivalry, love, and secret passwords.

These women loved each other, or argued bitterly; left their families, and returned; used fashion to secretly communicate with each other, or to win wars. They struggled with their bodies, journeyed far from home, wrestled with God. I felt I knew them, and I was grateful for their company in my life.

I was supposed to be writing my master's thesis about them, and the due date was fast approaching, but I found myself frozen. I had come to love these women, despite their mythic character, and couldn't bear the thought of trapping them on my laptop in what would have doubtless been a second-rate thesis paper, since I was (after all) an artist moonlighting in academia. So, as the deadline approached, Bartleby-like, I simply failed to begin writing.

The first time I gathered my courage and walked into my adviser's office to ask for an extension on my thesis, he signed the paper without question, barely looking up. A kind and brilliant rabbi with a good sense of humor, he knew me well; he'd even brought his wife to my bluegrass show at a bar downtown, feeling hip until (he laughed, recounting this the next day) someone asked him if he was my father.

When I slunk into his office two weeks later to request a second extension, he narrowed his eyes at me. "What's going on with you?" he asked, kindly, hands clasped on his desk.

I explained my problem, and he sighed. "Oh good," he said, shaking his head, "I was worried it was a *real* problem." He was silent for a minute, then his thick eyebrows suddenly lifted. "What if," he said slowly, "you wrote songs about your research instead of a paper? If you annotate them with references to the texts, I bet I can convince the dean to give you your degree."

That night, I sat cross-legged on my bed with my old beat-up Kay guitar, which I'd bought from a friend a couple years ago for two hundred dollars. He called it the "feral cat guitar," but it sat patiently on my lap, waiting for me to lead the way. After all these years prancing around with my violin, endless notebook pages filled with poems, I'd never combined words and music; I knew basic guitar chords, but had no idea how to write a song. There was nothing to do but let my fingers move and see what chords they found. I opened my mouth and thought, *What would I sing if I were Miriam, Vashti, Tamar?* A door opened in my chest. C chord, G chord. *My mother named me bitter,* I wrote, thinking of one etymology of Miriam's name, *although as a child I was so kind . . .*

I'd never been very good at Rubik's Cube, but the puzzle of songwriting immediately captivated me with its sense of interlocking combinations, trying one after the next until one clicked. I'd stare blankly at my bedroom wall as my fingers formed different chords in different orders, until I found a little gem, some combination of rhythm and chords that slotted together well. Sometimes I'd start with the music, mouthing random phrases as I worked out the melody, then turning my attention to the lyrics, finding the line word by word. Other times a string of lyrics would come to me—*If your father spit in your face, wouldn't you want to leave that place?*—just as my fingers would find the chords that supported them. Over and over I played each line, changing music or notes, phrasing or picking pattern, one variable and then another, until it snapped into place with certainty.

Once I'd learned to write on guitar, I missed my violin, so I learned to use a looping pedal. Plugging my violin pickup into the electronic pedal allowed me to layer melodies in real time, building increasingly complex orchestral textures alone with my instrument. Shyly, I started to play these songs onstage in short sets, sometimes inviting other musician friends to join me.

I'd grown used to performing onstage with Golem, and in that context, my shame at being held in the spotlight had abated to a level where I could ignore it. But now, testing out my songs about women in Torah in a loud bar, that shame came roaring back, along with crippling anxiety. On show days, I couldn't get any work done; I woke up with a stomachache, which grew worse and worse until the moment the performance ended, then magically disappeared.

Still, I felt that tractor beam: the irresistible pull of fear, challenge, going ever deeper into the cave where the real lessons were. I kept climbing the steps onstage in bars and singing my songs about biblical women, month after month. When a small Jewish record label invited me to put out an album, I wrote more story-songs, and my set expanded. I sang about the difficulty in these stories, the moments of loneliness and despair, the failure and shame.

At first the sound of my own voice was shocking and raw to me. But the more I sang through the masks of these ancient women who had come to feel like my friends, the more possible it became to keep singing. I learned these lessons of vulnerability night after night as I stood there, my mouth wide open, my heart undefended, held by the stage lights, the audience an invisible throbbing energy in the darkness before me. I called the project Girls in Trouble.

One of my teachers in yeshiva used to say that time is a spiral, and each year as we read the Torah again we round that circle again, one level higher. We add our own voice to all the other voices, and to the chorus of millions and millions who have sat with these stories, pondered them, listened to them, pushed back against them, made these myths their own. And we make a path forward for those who will interpret these stories after us.

I plugged my violin into my loop pedal, I held my guitar, I opened my mouth and sang these ancient stories. I could feel the beating heart in each story, the longing at the center of everyone. The risk, the danger, the bravery, the failure, the sheer vulnerability of being human. I felt myself, a vibrating dot on the spiral.

Leaving the Mythical Realm

Shellfish is not kosher; it had been years since I'd tasted it. But then I went to Venice.

Golem played a show in Paris, and instead of coming straight home, I found a cheap ticket to visit a friend who'd moved to Italy. I joined his circle for their five p.m. ritual: drinks together as the sun set, then dinner in the sparkling night. We sat together at a tiny restaurant just beside a canal, where the friends laughed and sang and slapped each other's backs. They ordered Aperol spritzes and a giant plate of *frutti di mare fritti* for the table. Our server brought a pile of delicate, freshly fried seafood, spread on a swath of brown butcher paper, and placed it on our small round table reverently, like an offering on an altar.

Scallops, mussels, tiny squid: fruit of the sea, none of it kosher. It smelled incredible, of oil and brine and the heat of an ancient oven. *I am alive,* I thought, as I lifted the crunchy tangled legs of the tiny octopus into my mouth, lights glittering on the dark surface of the water.

Perhaps it was the mellowing effect of leaving my twenties that shifted my relationship to Jewish practice. Or the increasing power music held over me, the way it began to feel again like my mother tongue. Or my decision not to join the rabbinate, which closed some doors and flung others open. But the rules that had once held me so reassuringly now began to chafe.

When I'd first moved back from Jerusalem, I was hungry for Jewish community and could not understand Eric's aversion to shul, to Shabbat dinners and communal events. Now, to my surprise, I began to feel it too: a resistance, like the push of two strong magnets rejecting each other's polarity.

I still loved teaching, the electric encounter with another person's soul. But the Shabbat table began to feel like a raft drifting slowly away from my center, and mid-meal I found myself longing for the easy, smoking-behind-the-high-school vibe of the music world. I began to dread what I had once loved: the taste of hummus and baba ghanoush on challah; the weekly exegesis of the Torah portion; the work of making it new, week after week.

I had been stretching the boundaries to the breaking point for a while—after all, performing on Saturdays was strictly forbidden, and I did it most weekends. But I had also been holding on to as many rules as I could; I strictly observed Shabbat on Friday nights, fasted on fast days, recited prayers as often as I could manage.

Now the thread was fraying. I began to turn from those structures that had held me so gently: the whispering and bowing and marking time, adapting my own actions to the sacred calendar. Little by little I left that beautiful four-dimensional quilt and reentered a life determined, once again, by the Gregorian calendar, by the schedules of my friends and family, by the patterns chords make when one follows another.

As I watched the Venetian friends' dinner ritual—their easy rapport, their fluency with a language I'd never speak—I thought back to my first visit to Shira's house on Rosh Hashanah. I remembered how at the holiday dinner table, I'd sat silent, watching the family's knowledge of Jewish traditions, so intuitive to them, so foreign to me. I remembered how it felt like I could almost see their understanding of the sacred, choreographed in the air around us—a dance, invisible but palpable. I hadn't understood the dance yet, but I'd felt more alive in its presence.

I'd felt called to learn that dance, movement by movement, and had been lucky enough to follow that calling.

But as I neared my thirtieth birthday, I began to realize that my true hunger was not for any particular system of rules; rather, it was the desire for that feeling—*I am alive.*

I'd always felt faintly mystified by the way my great-grandparents could throw away the whole system of laws and traditions they'd inherited, all that community, all those bonds. Now I found myself wondering: What if I just got up and walked away from the tables of singing Jews, out into the cold, lonely, galvanizing night?

"I'm ready to play on Friday nights," I told Annette when I came back to New York.

She tilted her head and regarded me, her religious fiddler, for a minute. "Are you sure?" she asked me.

"Yes." I nodded, and it was true.

And step by step, without fanfare, I followed that feeling, and it led me to a place where I could love the rules I had learned to inhabit, without feeling bound by them. I held the laws, those vessels for carrying holiness in time, and I let them fall to the floor and shatter, trusting that what was important would remain in my heart, a part of me now. My departure was gentle, like untangling a knot. I didn't suddenly begin to break all the rules that bind humans to the Divine; I simply allowed myself to change. I was alive.

I felt at once peaceful, and guilty. But my instinct turned out to be true: what was truly important to me remained. Each morning, I slipped my right shoe on first, since the right is the side of compassion. After a gig, when I crawled into bed and pulled my quilt over myself at two a.m., I whispered the Shema before I fell asleep, connecting with the unity of the Divine and remembering my own smallness. Looking at strangers on the subway, I saw the kabbalistic map of the *sefirot* and how energy coursed through their bodies, as it coursed through mine.

I continued to gather the stories of women of Torah around me, too, like a quilt to keep me warm. They reminded me over and over that my embarrassing personal struggles were not mine alone. Instead, they were timeless, human, and they connected me to women, and all humans, across the ages. *We had to learn that too,* they whispered into my ears when I needed them most. *You are not alone.* Hannah needed to find the courage to ask for her heart's desire. Vashti had to learn to love and honor her own boundaries in a world that wanted to control her. The Israelite women in Egypt had to find love and pleasure and sex even as the world churned around them, threatening their very survival.

At first I knew nothing and was hungry for rules to hold me. Then I learned the rules, and for a time was relieved to live inside them. But I kept changing, I kept growing, like a tree beneath concrete, unstoppable. I'd thought I understood my own story, but then the spiral had continued to unfurl inside me. This container that had felt so sacred and safe did not fit me anymore, though I still held love for it.

The end is always disguised as a beginning, the beginning as an end. Holding this tension, this liberation, this loss, I walked forward into time: once again unmarked, empty of invisible walls.

Torah in a Bar

I was perched on the edge of a worn purple couch at my neighborhood bar. I was there for my friend's birthday party, and I'd dressed up to celebrate, in a dark blue vintage dress with white piping, and two-inch navy-blue heels from the thrift shop down the street. I tried not to spill my glass of scotch on my lap as friends squished together on the couch, laughing and swapping life updates.

When my turn came, I mused out loud about the Girls in Trouble album I was planning to record. Writing these songs, I was realizing, meant joining the age-old interpretative tradition of midrash: reimagining ancient stories through the lens of my own time. But writing midrash in the form of songs raised particular questions: Should I lean toward folk, rock, or some combination? Would the arrangements be different for each song? And how many genres could fit in one album, anyway?

In my peripheral vision, I noticed a man with a scruffy beard listening intently as I spoke. Half jaunty hipster, half punk weirdo, he wore glasses and a worn T-shirt with a three-piece-suit vest, and his hair stuck straight up. I stopped talking and turned to him, a little annoyed—*Can I help you?*—and he met my gaze, his hazel eyes regarding me with what seemed to be amusement.

"Are you talking about midrash?" he said. I nodded. His eyes twinkled as he gestured to the room. "I mean . . . in a *bar*? Don't you think that's a little unusual?"

Since moving back to New York seven years ago, I'd signed up for dating sites, had a one-night stand with a man who worked for a record label, spent three glorious weeks with a woman in vet school. I'd sat in Prospect Park with a hipster guy who had grown up Orthodox, who scolded me when I said something about the Talmud, saying it wasn't sexy to talk about Talmud on a first date.

Now I took a beat and considered this stranger and his question. *Was* it unusual to talk about midrash in a bar? No, I decided, and said, "Not really," a bit more sharply than I meant to. "Where do you live?"

"Portland, Oregon."

"Well, welcome to Brooklyn," I said, "where we talk about Torah in bars."

Aaron, it turned out, was a bass player—Jewish, not observant—who had just finished a job tour-managing a friend's band across the country. A mutual friend had brought him to the party. We didn't exchange numbers, and I forgot about our conversation.

Then, a week later, a message notification appeared in Myspace. *You friend-requested my band!* he wrote. It's true; I had come across their profile and clicked "request," having no idea it was his band. *I was going to ask someone from the party to get me your number,* his message continued, *because I'm coming to New York in February, but now here you are! Have a drink with me?*

The timing was not great. His visit fell on the week of my thirtieth birthday, which happened to be Valentine's Day; I had a solo show that week, which meant hours of practicing and nervous stomachaches; plus, I had to get my apartment ready for the formal tea party I was throwing to celebrate my birthday.

Also, I was dating someone. In fact, I'd decided that part of building a container for me was practicing non-monogamy—retaining my essential independence, resisting the urge to collapse fully into any one person—so I was actually dating two people: a woman in Brooklyn and a man in California. Both lovely, deep-hearted souls, they were fine with this arrangement, and it technically wouldn't have been a problem to add a third, but what could I possibly need with a boyfriend in Portland? Still, I agreed to meet this scruffy bass player for a drink. What was the harm, he lived so far away, and it was so odd that I'd friend-requested his band without knowing it, and something in me told me to say yes.

Two months later, on the way out the door to meet Aaron on the eve of my thirtieth birthday, I made a promise to myself: I wouldn't try to be anyone other than who I was. I wouldn't laugh at a single joke I didn't find funny, wouldn't try to make myself any more palatable than I was. Dating as a practice of self-love.

He was handsomer than I'd remembered, and funny. And kind. When I said I loved poetry, he said earnestly, "Oh, I've never gotten poetry. Maybe you could help me understand it." After our second drink, I looked at my watch. The time had passed quickly; only an hour before midnight. On a whim, I turned to Aaron, and asked: "Do you want to be the last kiss of my twenties?"

He responded, "Huh?"

I would learn later that his hearing was impacted from years of touring. I had to repeat my quip, red-faced this time. And then he smiled widely, turned to face me, and put his hands on my shoulders.

I'd expected a casual kiss, but instead I felt a rush of overwhelming energy: the star-shaped "Wham!" of a comic book. Aaron sat back, hands on his knees, and looked at me with a combination of satisfaction and hunger, as if to say, *I told you so*. Then he placed his hand on the nape of my neck, pulling me in gently for another kiss.

It had begun to snow. After midnight, he walked me home on Seventh Avenue, as Brooklyn softened into silence. I slid my key into the heavy front door, stepped in, and held it open for him. He stayed that night, and the next, and again the night of my birthday party, where he bravely met most of the people I loved, all on one night.

The Talmud debates whether our partners are painstakingly sought out in this lifetime, or predestined. One rabbi says, *Making matches is as difficult for God as dividing the Red Sea.* Another counters, *Forty days before the creation of a child, a Heavenly issues forth and proclaims, This person will be matched with that person!*

Pragmatism and romance: at odds, and intimately connected. *Bashert,* the Yiddish word for "destined one" or "soulmate," is romantic; it comes not from Hebrew, but from Middle High German. The Talmud uses the more practical word *zivug,* akin to "partner." It seems an improbable miracle: to find a person, out of all the many people we encounter, who *matches* us in some fundamental way.

I am my beloved's, and my beloved is mine, says the Song of Songs. In the most commonplace way—a friend's birthday party, a bass player passing through town, a conversation overheard in a bar—life is forever transformed.

~

Beneath the chuppah, I walked seven circles around Aaron. We had asked my *chavruta* from Jerusalem to marry us. He was a rabbi now, long married to Emily. I'd read the ketubah at their wedding, and we'd kept in touch over the years; they'd even hosted me and Aaron for a house concert the year before, their adorable little kids sitting in the front row as we played.

Now, holding a silver cup of wine, my old *chavruta,* the rabbi, chanted in Hebrew: *Blessed are you, God, ruler of the universe, who has created humans in Your own image, out of Your own very Self, a perpetual fabric.*

Wine on my tongue, a sip of a potion. Words binding us together for life with their magic, like the spells I used to whisper over bowls of clover and ivy as a child.

Blessed are you, Adonai, creator of the vine.

My hands in his hands. His flecked with green and brown, the green of the forest surrounding us, the brown of earth, of which we are made and to which we will return. *Blessed are you, Adonai, who creates humans.*

Marriage. Bread, blood, fire. Now we were bound together until death by our hidden stories, our secret passwords.

∾

It's tempting to end the story here. To say I found love, and that love healed me, and I was home at last, in a container that fit. To tell you that together we built a happy family, with one parent who had fallen in love with the Divine, and one who was an atheist, and two little humans who would find their own paths one day.

I could show you how we lit the Shabbat candles together every week, Aaron handsome in his vest and glasses, hair still sticking up straight, as he poured grape juice into four kiddush cups; me wearing a green head wrap, humble before the majesty of the sacred as I struck the match and watched its flare reflected in my children's faces. How we each lifted up one child and held them, the four of us swaying together as we sang the blessings in the quiet moments just before Friday sunset.

All this would be true. But it wouldn't be the whole story.

I Had Thought I'd Return

I'd practically memorized the home-birth book my own mother had used to prepare before giving birth to me in Portland all those years ago; it lay on my bedside table at home, ready to support me when contractions began. But the birthing center had a strict time-out policy, I hadn't gone into labor in time, and although the baby was never in distress, they'd said I had no choice but to go to the hospital and into the operating room.

And so, my first night as a mother, I lay in a hospital bed recovering from an unexpected C-section at Maimonides Hospital, where no overnight guests were allowed, and mothers were not permitted to sleep holding their babies. I had to let the nurse take my newborn from me, swaddle her, and lie her down, face-up in a clear plastic bassinet, alone. I could visit her and nurse her, but I could not keep her in my bed and sleep. So I did not sleep, except for two-hour naps between visits.

After one of these naps, I awoke in the middle of the night and padded down the hospital corridor to get my baby. Outside the nursery, while I waited for the nurse to emerge with my daughter in her arms, I saw a framed kabbalistic blessing on the wall. Hebrew letters curved, forming the shape of two hands giving the priestly blessing. I stood there, my torso a swollen shell, looking at the letters which had followed me so far. *You've found me here, too,* I thought. *Thank you.*

We named our baby in our railroad apartment, her newly minted grandparents and aunts and uncles packed into the living room. The rabbi of the synagogue where I taught wrapped our newborn in a tallit, gently dotted her forehead with water, and together we welcomed her to the world with the name we had chosen: *Sylvia.*

But the three of us could not last in Brooklyn. Aaron had always wanted to move back to Oregon; newly vulnerable, recovering from surgery, I, too, longed for quiet and green. And raising a child as two artists in New York City seemed impossible; I turned the financial math over and over in my head, but I couldn't get it to work. The container was breaking, changing again.

A friend watched the baby in our empty apartment while we carried all our belongings two flights downstairs in boxes and loaded them onto a moving truck. We packed our suitcases and my violin and baby Sylvia in the car. And then we were gone, singing as we drove across the Verrazano-Narrows Bridge from Brooklyn to Staten Island. My life was changing radically already, I thought. Why not transform it wholly?

∾

And it was true that on the West Coast, I could breathe. But as soon as we had unpacked, I was seized with fear that I had made a terrible mistake. So much of what I had called my life was now three thousand miles away. Golem took the stage with their new fiddler, laughing, pushing the tempo faster beneath the bright lights, making the audience whirl and jump, while I walked numbly and alone through the streets of North Portland, pushing a stroller.

I found myself flattened with loneliness in this faraway land where I knew no one—not even myself, in this new mother-incarnation. The shining windows of Manhattan, the blurry silver walls of the subway, my own family, who knew my past and my present: all those surfaces that had reflected my own face back to me for so many years were now a world away. And I was no longer young, not in the way I had been. Starting over was getting harder.

~

There are some places a *bashert* and a baby cannot reach, no matter how much you love them.

A continent away from the place that had been home, and awash in the bleakness of postpartum despair, I came face-to-face with my greatest fear: my own loneliness. Since childhood I'd been running from that howling, freezing nothingness. The deepest reaches of outer space lived at my own core, and I'd tried to escape it over and over again. I hid in beautiful words and beautiful music. I hid in Shabbat dinners and devotional prayer and ecstatic study. I hid in late-night jam sessions at warm candlelit bars, and on tours where we played in a new city every night. I was always finding a way to distract myself from the terrifying chasm inside me.

On the boat I'd sailed on in college, we had learned about the blind fish who live seven miles beneath the surface of the ocean, where there is no light, and therefore no need to see. I thought of these fish often in those days, when I went so deep into this loneliness that my body grew numb with cold. I closed my eyes and my frozen toes touched the murky bottom. I was so angry at myself for following love to this cold place, sometimes I wondered if I should stop breathing.

Then, slowly, I began to find that I could exist down there, too.

I don't know how to say it any other way: it was like breathing underwater, a letting go of the way I'd lived. Past the pain was a sort of no-feeling, which opened into the beginning of a strength I hadn't known was there.

I began to understand, after all these years of trying to run from the pain of being human, that I had another choice. Instead of trying to escape, I could face my own most profound fear—my own essential aloneness—and survive. Like Miriam, exiled in the desert. Or Ruth, walking out into the field at night in a land where she knew no one. Or Vashti, living out the rest of her life after being sent away from the palace for speaking her truth. I could keep myself company.

∾

If you've ever propagated a plant in water on a windowsill, you've seen how roots grow. White tendrils reach their way down, searching to anchor: they find what is needed, draw the nourishment up, bind the plant to this world, keep it alive.

In this way, I began to rebuild. I woke up each morning, played with the baby, drank coffee. I taught twelve-year-olds to chant Torah. I wrote poems no one would read. The garden boxes overflowed with lavender and sage. I rescued rosebushes and a weeping cherry tree our neighbors had dug up from their yard and I planted them in ours, too close together, where they grew in a riot of pinks and oranges and reds.

In the corner of the yard we built a little green shed with yellow trim, a claw-foot tub hidden behind it. A place for music and for teaching. We called it the Torah Hut.

Sometimes I'd be invited to play a Girls in Trouble show on the East Coast, and Aaron would join me on bass. We boarded the plane, juggling our instruments and our baby. During sound check, we took turns wearing Sylvia in a carrier, strapped to our back, the vibrations of our instruments traveling through our bodies into hers.

One summer Sunday, I sat at home in a patch of sunlight on the floor with my guitar. Sylvia was crawling in circles around me, and I was writing a song about Lot's wife, and how hard it was to leave a place you loved—whether Sodom or New York City—even if you knew it was time. Sylvia stopped crawling and smiled at me, her balloon-taut cheeks growing even larger. I thought of my Bible teacher at yeshiva, the one who used to pinch his own cheeks rather than mine.

The melody had a jagged part that jumped high, then low, repeatedly. Sylvia grinned, and cooed, and then began to mimic the pitches of my song with her own coos: up and down, up and down. She was singing for the first time. She would find her own voice, too, I thought. Her own beauty, her own loneliness, her own way of living with all of it.

∾

I gave birth to a son. My roots grew deeper into the soil. My hair grew more gray. The current of time carried me farther away from my youth and closer to the old woman inside me, the one who appeared to my teenaged self so long ago, looking lovingly back from the mirror. I'm halfway between the two now, and finally ready to accept that the solid stopping place I once longed for was an illusion. That perhaps the only real home, sanctuary on earth, is the constancy of change, the never-ending spiral.

Ratzo v'shov. Being alive is a fabric, woven endlessly, back and forth. Even death becomes a part of that tapestry. What is home becomes foreign, what is foreign turns into home.

And even this home, this land where I live, does not belong to me; I live on stolen land. But what place on earth, for a person like me, is not stolen land?

Nowhere belongs to me. But I belong to a few places.

There's the house in which I grew up, where *The Garden of Earthly Delights* hung on the wall, signaling another layer of existence beyond the one we could see. And New York City, where everyone is unique and no one is unusual. And every *beit midrash* in the world, anywhere the letters of the Torah throb and pulse, even the spaces that would not welcome my presence as a woman.

Like so many of my ancestors before me, I am forged by the diaspora, and diaspora is where I make my home. Here I raise my children and teach my students and rosin my bow. Here I slowly learn to love myself, and to discern what I need, and how to have the courage to ask for it—or simply make it happen, like those complicated women of the Bible I have come to love so well: imperfect, messy, real.

I begin to ask anew, as the spiral turns again: What does it mean to receive an ancient tradition, and make it our own? What does it mean to carry the past into the future? To balance receiving with creating?

Here in the diaspora I braid what I was given, what I have sought to learn, and what I begin to create. Words of English and Hebrew and Aramaic, my fingertips pressing the string down onto the neck of the violin, my body pressed against the one I love, moonlight illuminating the challah crumbs scattered across the dining room table, kids' toys on the floor, holy books on the shelves, a garden full of sage and rosemary, trees outside the window holding nights and days in their green needles.

Here the moon draws her figure eight in the sky, over and over, for as many months as I am lucky to be alive on this earth, to which I belong.

Lilith

When I first learned of Lilith, winged night bird, First Eve, mystical proto-feminist, I felt a thrill. And I am not the first. She has continued to fly through the human imagination over cultures, centuries, and continents. She is unrepentant, fierce, fiery. She holds herself in high regard.

Lilith does not appear in the Torah itself, giving her the spooky status of "apocryphal." Her origins seem to lie in a Sumerian storm-demoness named Lilitu, who was incorporated into the superstitions of ancient Israelite culture. And yet, despite being a mysterious creature without a clear link in our oldest texts, Lilith's legend has been carried forward for millennia, interpreted differently in different ages.

To follow Lilith's journey is to experience a prism of relationships to female power. The Jewish mystics imagined Lilith as a proto-Eve, the First Woman, banished from Eden for considering herself equal to Adam—in some versions, for wanting to be on top during sex. And so God drives Lilith from the garden and starts over with Eve, created from Adam's body to make sure we understand that she is (we are) secondary.

For centuries afterward, Lilith lives in the Israelite imagination as a cosmic baby-killer and succubus, consort of a demon, furious at her banishment from Eden. Medieval Jews mutter incantations against her at the most intimate moments of their lives, from sex to childbirth. Then, in the 1970s, a dramatic swerve: Lilith is reclaimed by feminists, and her name proudly given to a secular women's music festival, as well as the first Jewish feminist magazine.

I love the contemporary trend of embracing and celebrating Lilith as a powerful woman. And yet I am equally drawn to the dangerous Lilith, to the amulets that pregnant and birthing women used to protect themselves against her. In these older, superstitious cultures, Lilith gives a name and a form to the deep human fears.

These fears are so deep precisely because of the strength of our love; they are the inverse measure of how precious life is, and how tenuous. The sexual, the familial, and the intensity of our responsibility to create and safeguard the next generation—all these twine together in her character. Even at her most demonic, Lilith reflects back to us the sweetness of what we love.

My Lilith has her boundaries; she will not return to the Garden in a world that will not recognize her power. But she will not stop looking, looking, looking for that home where she can be exactly who she is, and be beloved once more.

What if each of us could learn to be our own version of this winged night-spirit, this unapologetic self, beyond categorization or naming?

What if we could hold ourselves in high regard, accepting ourselves fiercely, knowing that we know we are enough, just as we are?

Maybe then we could take the power that would create inside us—the energy, the radiance—and, in loving ourselves, fill the world with love.

Epilogue: A Ritual

Most of my b'nai mitzvah students show up for their first lesson with the same expression on their faces I must have had at their age: curious, a little nervous, proud to be old enough to begin. Sometimes we meet in the Torah Hut in my yard—more often, these days, we regard each other through our glowing computer screens. Either way, we face each other, we recite the blessing celebrating beginnings, and then my work begins.

I do my best to hand them the keys to our tradition, one by one. *See these symbols—this squiggle, this curve? They're called trope. They tell us how to chant the words of your portion.*

Together we trace signs in the air, stringing notes and syllables together until they add up to ancient stories. We discuss the stories, and I watch each student's expression transform as she realizes she is allowed to criticize the characters, to argue with God. *Sometimes the Torah teaches us how to live,* I tell them. *And sometimes it just helps us remember that being human is complicated.*

After a year of weekly lessons, I stand beside my student in front of their family and community—in a ballroom, a backyard, a rented rock club, an urban farm, a forest—as they chant from the Torah, and we celebrate their passage across the bridge from childhood to the very beginning of adulthood.

~

Once or twice a year, when my family went to synagogue, I would trace the Hebrew letters in the prayer book slowly with my fingertips. I'd been taught how to pronounce them but not what they meant. I wondered about the resonant, oceanic depths I sensed beneath those syllables; that wondering would lead me across the world and back.

Now my daughter is eleven; it's almost time for her to begin studying for her own bat mitzvah. I offered to teach her, but she widened her eyes in alarm and shook her head. No, of course not; she has to find her own path, as I had to find mine.

~

This I know: In the midst of grocery shopping and news, of dirty laundry and to-do lists and the internet, we have ritual. I don't believe this ritual should be punishing, or forced. I believe it should be there for us when we need it. To hold us; to carry us. To help us remember that magic is woven through the everyday like a thread of gold, and if we stop for a moment, we can find it.

And we have tools, different for each of us. I have my violin, which turns the air around me into stained glass; my attention, shining love onto my students exactly where they are; and texts written two thousand years ago, which my tongue has turned over and over until they are smooth as a stone.

Together we tap into the groundwater of divinity that runs beneath us, the constellations above us, the mysterious electricity that lives inside us.

∾

Where does a story begin: When you fall in love, or when you leave? When you learn to write the first letter of an ancient alphabet, or when you learn to forget the ancient rules and whisper the words of your own heart?

The mystics say that the state of being alive is *ratzo v'shov*, to run and return. We run to God, drawn to the fire of holiness, to change our lives, to refine ourselves; we run to each other, to tear our clothes off and fall down together, forgetting everything that came before. And then we return to ourselves, turning away from God, from the lover, back home to our own particular body, our story, limits, needs.

Run and return and run again.

∾

According to the rabbis, an angel teaches us the entire Torah in the womb. Swimming in that amniotic darkness, a candle burning overhead, we hold all the wisdom in the world.

If they're right, to be born is to let all that wisdom go. Then we spend the rest of our lives learning it again, letter by letter.

Acknowledgments

With humble gratitude to the Divine; to you, reader; and to the many, many people without whom this book would not exist:

To my dream agent, Jennifer Thompson, at Nordlyset: thank you for seeing the heart and soul of this book so clearly, and guiding it into the world with such grace and groundedness. Thanks also to Isabelle Bleecker at Nordlyset.

It is a profound honor to be published by Schocken Books, which has published so many of my spiritual and literary inspirations. To my incredible editor, Anna Kaufman, and the wonderful Natalia Berry: thanks for your care, and for your thoughtful, brilliant, insightful edits (which were also, somehow, laugh-out-loud funny?!). Gratitude also to the entire Schocken team: editorial director Ben Hyman, production editor Ellen Feldman, copy editor Karen Thompson, proofreaders Judy Kiviat and Carol Rutan, text designer Cassandra Pappas, jacket designer Janet Hansen, publicists Tricia Cave, Kelly Shi, and Moshe Schulman, and marketer Ellen Whitaker.

Deep thanks to writer compadres Rebecca Clarren, Vanessa Hua, Jesse Lichtenstein, David Naimon, Daniel Pollack-Pelzner, Moshe Schulman, Justin Taylor, and Jay Aquinas Thompson, and dear artist friend Jen P. Harris, for hours of precious (and occasionally agonized) conversations about the writing life, across many miles of walks and hikes, over many beverages, for many years.

To decades-beloved poet friends Kate Angus and Filip Marinovich, I bow to each of you. And thanks to Ross White and the volunteers who administer the Grind, which keeps so many of us up in each other's first drafts, and helped me write this book.

To the generous and wise writer friends from whom I received notes on previous drafts of this book over the past ten or so years, thank you! Lacking faith this day would come, I didn't keep a list, so I am certain I will forget to name some people here; to paraphrase Roger Reeves, please charge these omissions to my head and not my heart. Writers who offered precious feedback on earlier drafts of this book (in addition to those already named above) include: Liz Asch, Susanna Childress, Nadia Colburn, Harmony Holiday, Leanne Lieberman, Cari Luna, Heather Sommerlad, Marcela Sulak, Michael Tallon, Chrys Tobey, Vandoren Wheeler, and Sara Wolkenfeld.

To my longtime musician friends—Annette Ezekiel Kogan, Aaron Diskin, Michael Daves, David Freeman, Taylor Bergren-Chrisman, Tim Monaghan, Curha, Dan Saks, and many more—I love you. Love also to my State Street beloveds—Megan, Dillon, and Kendra—and to my moon women: Becca, Hannah, Michal, Sonya. And to Malinda Ray Allen for all these years of figuring shit out together.

Profound thanks to Jane Gottesman for the ongoing treasure of friendship, deep conversation, and sacred world-building together, and love to the whole Biddle-Gottesman family. I am grateful that the tapestries of our lives continue to interweave.

Gratitude to Penelope Rose Miller for holding space for creative manifestation over many hours in your sacred coaching shed, and also to Michelle MacAleese, Temim Fruchter, Diana Spechler, and Jill Rothenberg, whose editorial suggestions helped me profoundly at critical moments in the writing of this book. And to my wise and generous rabbinic ordination team (b"h)—a story for another book!—Rabbi Ellen Lippmann, Rabbi Or Rose, Rabbi Benay Lappe.

Miriam Altshuler: thank you for your generous mentorship during the early years of my desperate attempts to figure out what it means for a poet to write prose, and for your insightful notes. Julie Barer: though I'm certain you don't remember this, thank you for coming up to me and saying, "You should try writing nonfiction," after a poetry reading; you planted the seed of this book.

Gratitude to Dr. Rabbi Burt Visotzky, for suggesting I write songs about biblical women during my time studying at the Jewish Theological Seminary, and for ongoing mentorship since; to Aaron Bisman, for helping those first self-recorded demos grow into Girls in Trouble, back in the JDub days; to Joni Blinderman Levine, for believing in me; to all my Covenant family colleagues, in particular the Beit HaYotzer folks; and to the extended Girls in Trouble creative family over the past fifteen-plus years— especially Alicia J. Rose, Lara Cuddy, Nessa Norich, Zak Margolis, and Ethan Chessin, and all the artists who have played on my albums and joined me onstage. Thanks also to everyone who has made touring possible by hosting shows, lending me guitars, letting me sleep on your couch, making me coffee, and welcoming me to your communities.

Rabbi Chanina said: "Much have I learned from my teachers, even more have I learned from my peers, but from my students I have learned more than from anyone else" (Talmud, Taanit 4a). To my teachers of Torah, music, and poetry—too many to name at this point—I am eternally grateful. Thank you for educating me with such love, compassion, and dedication and for welcoming me into the various guilds in which I serve. What can I do but attempt to give my own students the gifts you have given me? I am grateful to my three-person ordination team, for being there to guide me when I finally received the call to become a rabbi. And to my students, Rabbi Chanina speaks the truth. Thank you for the privilege of learning from you.

I am grateful to have received invaluable support for the creation and editing of this book from the Peleh Fund and the Covenant Foundation. Thanks also to the Sefaria-Maharat Writing Circle (Gila Fine, Batya Hefter, Malka Simkovich, Sara Wolkenfeld, and others). The gift of time and space from the Peleh Family Residency, in Berkeley, enabled a critical revision. For focused space to write in Portland, I am grateful to the Writers Block workspace, to Andrea Cohen for the mini-residency, and to The Stacks Coffeehouse in North Portland, one of my favorite places to write. Shout out to Mary Milstead, for holding space, and to Jackson, for years of good vibes.

Thanks to the editors of the publications in which excerpts from this book appeared, often in different versions: Awst Press's online essay series (special thanks to Tatiana Ryckman and Sophronia Scott), *Lilith,* and *The Forward.*

To everyone who appears in these pages, I ask your forgiveness for anything that contradicts the way you remember things, or would have wished to be written about. אנא סלח לי

To Avniel z"l, who taught me so much of what I know, whose presence blessed this world for too short a time—thank you for everything.

To my parents, Peter and Karen, and my sisters, Stephanie and Nora: I hit the family jackpot, being born into this one. Thank you for rolling with me through everything described in this book (and much more). I love you more than I can say.

To Aaron, my beloved, my באשערט. Though (as you like to point out) your word count in this book is a little low, my love for you is deep and true, and extends past the edges of the universe. Thank you for being the first person to hear many of these passages in our late-night memoir-swap sessions, reading out loud to each other on the couch when our kids were still little. Thank you for music, words, laughter, joy, and realness. And thank you for sharing this life with me, the greatest blessing.

To Sylvia גלילה and Elijah אליהו נחמן—my loves, my everything. Thank you for making me a mother. May the Divine bless you and keep you as you forge your own paths through this world. I love both of you forever and ever and ever, amen selah.

A NOTE ABOUT THE AUTHOR

ALICIA JO RABINS is a writer, musician, performer, and Torah teacher. She is the author of *Divinity School* (winner of the APR/Honickman First Book Prize) and *Fruit Geode* (finalist for the Jewish Book Award), and of the collection of personal essays *Even God Had Bad Parenting Days.* Rabins is the creator and star of *A Kaddish for Bernie Madoff,* an independent feature film about the intersection of finance and mysticism, which *The Atlantic* calls "a blessing." As a musician, she has released three albums (and accompanying feminist study guides) with her indie-folk song cycle about biblical women, *Girls in Trouble.*

A NOTE ON THE TYPE

This book was set in Minion, a typeface produced by the Adobe Corporation specifically for the Macintosh personal computer and released in 1990. Designed by Robert Slimbach, Minion combines the classic characteristics of old-style faces with the full complement of weights required for modern typesetting.

Typeset by Scribe, Philadelphia, Pennsylvania

Designed by Cassandra J. Pappas